FREEI
ANI
IMMORTALITY⊙

D1649322

33.7
RAM

by the same author

CHRISTIAN ETHICS AND CONTEMPORARY PHILOSOPHY

RELIGIOUS LANGUAGE

WORDS ABOUT GOD
editor

FREEDOM
AND
IMMORTALITY

The Forwood Lectures
in the
University of Liverpool
1957

IAN T. RAMSEY

SCM PRESS LTD
56 BLOOMSBURY STREET
LONDON

334 00499 3
First published 1960
by SCM Press Ltd
56 Bloomsbury Street London
Second impression 1971

© SCM Press Ltd 1960

Printed in Great Britain by
Fletcher & Son Ltd, Norwich

CONTENTS

The apparently profitless and unending discussion of predictability serves to reveal two opposing viewpoints: that human behaviour is, and is not, respectively, merely a matter of what is in principle observable; that 'acts of will' are, and are not, respectively, 'objects'.

These two views traditionally characterised the approaches of science and morality respectively: moralists have claimed that a 'free choice' or a 'responsible decision' contains something more than the behaviour changes that are to be observed.

Yet Libertarianism fails as an attempt to say what is peculiar about a 'responsible decision'.

Four examples to illustrate the character of a 'free' decision and to show that the diversity of the ordinary language we use, and the ordinary situations it describes is such as can recognise and allow for the 'free will' claim that in a moment of decision, a man realises himself to be not only the behaviour he displays to scientific observation, but 'more' as well. The best 'arguments' for free will are the kinds of situation to which these examples are meant to call attention.

Retrospect.

Three examples suggest that a 'free' decision is rightly seen as a 'response', a response to a peculiar challenge we call 'moral obligation' and which is the challenge of 'objects' and more.

More examples of 'plain' and 'responsible' decisions to make clearer this transcendent reference which makes the challenge 'moral'.

The complete doctrine of free will is a claim that

there are certain situations in which *subjectively* a person transcends his public behaviour, acts more than 'officially'; and that this occurs as a response to a challenge which in the same way but *objectively* transcends any 'observables', though it is expressed through them. Such a challenge we call 'obligation'.
Three corollaries:

To justify 'freedom' by appealing to decision situations which exceed public behaviour, and even to recall our use of nicknames, is to see in principle how to justify belief in immortality.

Typical arguments *against* immortality endeavour to avoid or to deny the kind of situation which (we would argue) is the empirical basis for immortality.

Typical arguments *for* immortality can all be viewed as techniques to evoke a more-than-objects, more-than-public-behaviour, kind of situation:

If belief in immortality is empirically grounded in the kind of situation we have been specially elucidating in Chapter III, what have we to say about the language used to talk about it?

What account can we give of 'immortality', 'unending life', 'eternal life'?

The 'Timeless Self' and 'Pure Ego'.

The treatment now broadens into a discussion of the Immortality of the Soul. We examine some unreliable guides to the logical behaviour of the word 'soul' and on these grounds question the significance of some theological theories such as Creationism or Traducianism. More positively, we suggest that the 'immortality of the soul' is best expressed as 'the immortality of I', noting that this suggestion well accords with Hebraic talk about the soul, though it is not so familiar a point of view in the Greek-Latin Scholastic tradition.

V. LANGUAGE ABOUT IMMORTALITY: A 'FUTURE' LIFE

All doctrines of a 'future' life have their logical basis in the fact that a never-ending sequence of observables – such as talk of an endless future life supplies – is one way of representing and portraying an immortality situation which is 'observables' and more besides. We then proceed to formulate certain distinguishable logical areas in discourse about a future life:

(I) The derivation of the concept of a continuous future and its subsequent replacement by the concept of *discontinuous* time-periods.

(II) A. Language of *continuity* supplemented by talk of an 'End'.

B. Language of *continuity* using as a basic language:

(i) language about purposiveness,
(ii) language about moral retribution,
(iii) language about personal affection.

Summary of arguments so far in this chapter.

Finally there follows a brief consideration of related topics:

(*a*) Pre-existence
(*b*) Is everyone immortal? Universalism
(*c*) Distinctively Christian claims

Retrospect.

VI. RETROSPECT

Brief summary of the main conclusions of the book.

ACKNOWLEDGMENTS

THOSE who honoured me with an invitation to deliver the Forwood Lectures added to the honour many unforgettable kindnesses in a place to which I was already affectionately bound by countless family ties. I have the liveliest memories of the hospitality of the Vice-Chancellor, Sir James Mountford, of Professor Fairman, Dean of the Faculty of Arts, and of his colleagues in the faculty, of the Dean of Liverpool, Dr Dillistone, and of the Chavasse Society.

But to Professor and Mrs Porteous in particular I am permanently indebted for the way they received me into their family and spared nothing for my welfare. They even showed to the lectures the same generosity as they extended to me.

Between the lectures and this book has come the patient endurance of my family and my secretary, Mrs Shaw, and no list of martyrs can close without a mention of them. I only hope that no reader will feel bound to complain that the list should have remained open at least long enough to include him, too.

INTRODUCTION

IT MAY SEEM very surprising to some readers that these not obviously similar themes of freedom and immortality should be brought together in one brief book. But for others the title perhaps stirs memories of Immanuel Kant, for whom immortality, freedom, and the existence of God, were (as he called them) postulates of pure practical reason. By this he meant, very roughly, that while it would be impossible to justify belief in immortality, freedom and the existence of God, if we were restricted to that kind of experience which can justify the concepts and principles used in the natural sciences, yet on a wider view of experience these beliefs could nevertheless be given a reasonable justification. While, as he claimed to show in his *Critique of Pure Reason*, such theological beliefs could not be established by reference to sense-experience alone, their significance nevertheless begins to be seen when we broaden our view-point and consider those situations where we are aware of moral obligations. Belief in God, freedom and immortality, could, in one way or another, be grounded in morality, and to show this was part of Kant's task in the *Critique of Practical Reason*. Though neither 'God' nor 'freedom' nor 'immortality', said Kant in effect, could ever be words native to scientific discourse, yet if we consider what is involved in responding to the claims of duty, then we begin to see how to use language about God or freedom or immortality, and the kind of justification which such language can be given.

Though I shall say little more about Kant, I am bold to think that his broad claim was reliable. What I hope to show is that these two topics of freedom and immortality are properly united because each makes a similar sort of claim about the universe; because each appeals to a similar kind of situation, a situation not restricted to the 'observables' of sense-experience. Further, at a time when we are being asked to show what it is that metaphysics and philosophical theology can have for their subject-matter when they are not mere verbiage or word spinning, I am bold to think that this limited discussion has a wider relevance. For I believe that the kind of situation which justifies belief in freedom and immortality, is the kind of situation to which we must appeal if we seek an empirical justification for the language of metaphysics and philosophical theology in general.

In this book, then, I approach from two directions, the one a consideration of freedom and the other a consideration of immortality, the kind of situation without reference to which the language of metaphysical theology will be logically compromised and vacuous. So behind all my discussion is the hope that while it centres on these two particular topics of freedom and immortality it will enable the reader to see the sort of defence which could be given to many traditional concepts, whether in metaphysics or philosophical theology, by someone who nevertheless wishes to give full credit to the approach and techniques of contemporary empiricism.

I

FREEDOM: PREDICTABILITY AND DECISION

WE SHALL centre our discussion of freedom around two themes, and these will be dealt with in Chapters I and II respectively. In this chapter we shall try to get clear what people are talking about when they say that they decided 'freely' to do so-and-so; we shall try to clarify what is meant by a 'free decision'. Thereafter in Chapter II we shall try to discover the connection between freedom and moral obligation; we shall try to see what is involved in the claim that I must be 'free' if I am to do my duty; in the claim that only if we are 'free' can a moral obligation be genuine.

Central to many discussions of the problem of free will has been the question of predictability, and I propose to start with an examination of the traditional treatment of this topic in order to spotlight the conflicting claims which the traditional discussion always enshrines, though it does not often make evident. I have no wish merely to repeat traditional claims or counter-claims as such, nor to develop them even further along the same lines. What I want to do instead is to look at the way the problem of free will has been traditionally treated so as to become clearer about the character of the opposing views which have expressed themselves in the various claims and counter-claims. So many discussions of freedom become such a bewildering interplay of claims and counter-claims that they seem to confuse rather than to clarify the problem. In filtering out claim and counter-claim I hope I may have better success.

On the one hand, we have been told, human behaviour is so very predictable that it must be determined. How could any transport system be arranged; how could *Bradshaw's Railway Guide* be compiled; how could shops lay in adequate stocks of food supplies, clothing and furniture, and so on, if the behaviour of travellers or customers was a pure matter of chance?

There then arises the counter-argument. It is pointed out that often the transport system is taken by surprise. Ten families with forty children between them, all happen to go out for the same bus to the Zoo, producing strife and disappointment. Again, how often does the seasoned traveller find Bradshaw's predictions accurately fulfilled? Or, for that matter, do we always find ice-cream at the kiosk in the park, or the cloth we want at our local tailor's?

But to counter these difficulties there is a very easy comeback. The transport system breaks down, we are told, only because it had not reckoned with cause-factors such as Mr O'Reilly winning the Pools and treating all the families in the neighbourhood on an afternoon's outing. *Bradshaw's Railway Guide* is only erroneous when certain cause-factors, such as the inability of a certain load of coal to produce steam, have been omitted from the argument. There is no ice-cream at the kiosk in the park because the supplier's knowledge of atmospheric cause-factors is so inadequate that they could not possibly predict the unexpectedly hot spell. There is at the moment none of that plain grey flannel in the local tailor's because the headmaster of a large school in the district, under pressure from his new wife, suddenly decided last term to change all his boys' clothing from blue suits to grey flannel; and can we reasonably expect the shopkeeper or his suppliers to reckon with a headmaster becoming unexpectedly married to a sartorially insistent wife? In all these ways, it is said, if only we had the wisdom to know all the cause-factors, behaviour would be completely predictable, everything would be determined, and we should discover that man is in fact without freedom. That is one story.

On the other hand it has been said that human behaviour is

so very unpredictable that it cannot possibly be completely determined. There is the confirmed bachelor who suddenly marries, to the astonishment of his friends. There is the Cabinet Minister whose resignation startles the country.

But, as before, there is a counter-argument. We may be surprised about the bachelor's marriage (it is said) but in fact we never saw him much between each Friday night and the following Monday morning. We never realised how he had been spending his week-ends for the last five years. Or again, we may be surprised about the Cabinet Minister, but in fact he has been telling his wife for years that he was becoming more and more ashamed of having to make the Party speeches which had been written for him.

At this stage there is, as before, a come-back. 'We quite agree', someone may say, 'that we do not know as much about the bachelor as we might have done. Even so, it does not account for his getting married to just this girl at just this time.' Or: 'I can appreciate that point about the Cabinet Minister, but it still doesn't account for his resignation coming just after his pro-motion in the Cabinet.' With such a come-back as this, the argument is now suggesting that no one can possibly account for all the details of every human situation once these are made sufficiently precise. Human behaviour is, in the last resort, and in all its detailed complexity, unpredictable and free.

Here then seems to be an impasse. But let us look more closely at the general character of the argument. Let us consider a situation S for whose occurrence certain cause-factors have, on any showing, combined and been relevant. Two points about S are important:

1. We can never specify S completely down to the last detail. Nor is that a difficulty we might with care and ability overcome. As long as space and time are characterised by infinite divisi-bility, there is always the possibility of being more precise. We can never exhaust all the possible features of any situation. Someone in 1969 may predict that a Cambridge landlady A will give an undergraduate B, belonging to College C, four

sausages for breakfast on Advent Sunday 1970. But will they specify exactly what kind of sausages? What percentage of meat? Of bread? What about the skin? And the next move, what sort of flour will have gone to make the bread, just what vitamins are present and in what quantity, how much added protein? and so on and so on. As soon as our expert on prediction has accounted for one feature, there is another awaiting an explanation, and meanwhile the enthusiast for unpredictability grows more confident.

2. But on the other hand we can never enumerate all the cause-factors which have been involved in the occurrence of S. This task, like the other, is equally unending. There is always some factor of which we shall find we have omitted to take account. Someone might say, for instance, that they well knew that the bachelor had spent his week-ends in such and such a way at his country cottage, but they *still* cannot imagine why he married. Why didn't he just continue the week-ends? Is not marriage utterly different from any number of week-end fun-fairs? 'Certainly,' the answer will be, 'but this only shows that we must not omit to take account of all the financial and social aspects of the marriage, the desire for a family and so on, and all these have cause-factors which must be investigated and revealed.' And if, when all these have been given cause-histories, there are still some features of the situation unaccounted for, there is always the unconscious to call in as a never-failing ally. The unconscious is a never-failing store of objects – unconscious desires, emotions, cravings – each of which can whet the appetite for more predictability.

The conclusion is, then, that unpredictability seems to arise only because we are too easily content with a restricted number of cause-factors. In the same way (we have seen) predictability may seem to arise when we are too easily content with an imperfect description of a certain situation.

So the controversy takes on a permanent character. On the one hand, if we begin by thinking that all human behaviour is predictable, we can always continue that argument against any opposition by appealing to cause-factors which have been over-looked. On the other hand, if we begin by arguing that human behaviour is unpredictable we can always continue that argument against any opposition by appealing to more and more specific features of some particular case.

What we have filtered out from this discussion of predictability, then, are two positions. The one view would claim that human behaviour, being something completely determined by antecedent cause-factors, is no more than its scientific features. The other view would claim that someone's actual behaviour, at a particular time, somehow eludes complete description in such terms. In considering human behaviour, the one approach concentrates wholly on causal antecedents; the other approach concentrates more and more on the particular behaviour being manifested. Nor, as we have seen, is it just a case of being unable to prove one or disprove the other. We can go on with either as long as we wish. Each is waving a different flag. Each is repeating a different key-phrase by which to understand the world. Each has a conviction which can always be supported by arguments and which is resistent to counter-arguments. For one, 'Everything is predictable.' For the other, 'Something about a concrete case of human behaviour is unpredictable.' The one is devoted to a growing pattern of external events; what is not known now will be known tomorrow; there is here no ultimate mystery. The other is devoted to something here and now about which there is the conviction that no story about causal events will ever be adequate to it. The one, we may remark in passing, is a purely natural devotion – it is often given the name of 'scientific humanism'. The other is a devotion which while being based on natural events includes something more as well – it is a characteristically 'religious' devotion, one not exhausted by the spatio-temporal objects it includes.

Another rough and ready way of expressing the difference between the two views is to say that they characterise broadly the traditional approaches of scientists and moralists respectively. At any rate, this reflection usefully reminds us that very often in the past the problem of free will has been said to be a problem of science *versus* morality – that science could not allow for freedom, whereas morality demanded it. Let us look a little further at this distinction between science and morality, in an endeavour to clarify and develop the two different stand-points and approaches which meet together in the problem of free will, and which it is our present purpose to separate out and to distinguish.

On the one hand, we have the scientific approach. It used to be said that science works on an ideal of complete determinism; whereupon a useful model for all the transactions of the universe is the billiard table. Suppose one billiard ball A_1 is set in motion with a velocity V_1 in a certain direction, and hits another ball B_1 at rest. The subsequent motions of the balls can then be completely determined once certain background factors are known, such as the coefficients of restitution of the balls, the friction of the cloth, and so on. If we go further back we shall of course, for a full story, need to take into account the impulse given to A_1 by the billiard cue, an impulse which (we shall be told) is equivalent to the force applied times the distance of application. What now if we go to the billiard player who decides to hit the ball? Even here, says the scientific approach, there is no difference in principle. All that this means is that we must now extend our causal field to include cause-factors belonging to the physiology and psychology of the billiard player. The picture of a completely determined area has been merely extended and complicated. The act of will is a spatio-temporal event as much as the movement of the billiard ball. Why then should it fall outside scientific treatment?

Nor let anyone at this juncture start whispering in our ears the name of Heisenberg. Let no one suggest that because in the usual way of talking we can never at one and the same time claim to know both 'the position' and 'the velocity' of an electron, then the scientific picture is imprecise enough to allow for some exceptional places for 'acts of will'. There is no hope along these lines. The scientific picture may no longer be constructed in terms of a *single* causation pattern which is *universal*, and this diversification with a sort of poetic licence may be expressed in ordinary language in terms of uncertainties. But even if scientific method has to work with the idea of many causal areas (and the most recent developments seem to suggest that this is by no means inevitable), human behaviour would still be no more than a complex of spatio-temporal events each with its causal ancestry, though now the causal ancestry would be extremely diverse, far more so than was at one time supposed. Further, we shall always be wise to avoid jumping to conclusions based on poetic paraphrases of scientific procedures.

Here then is the scientific approach, with human behaviour and 'acts of will' understood wholly in terms of spatio-temporal events[1]; what may be called alternatively 'observables' or merely 'objects'.

There is on the other hand the approach of morality. It is often said that if I am to show responsible behaviour, if I am to make a responsible decision, I must be free to choose between alternatives. I think this can be put less vaguely by saying that for something to be my duty, I must be able to avoid it. Whatever else 'ought' does or does not imply, it certainly implies 'need not', so that to do my duty, to respond to some obligation, calls for at least a simple decision between two alternatives – doing something or avoiding it. On the basis of these considerations it is said that to do my duty demands the freedom of being able to actualise one or other of at least two alternatives. We must not be 'compelled' to do one of them.

Even so, I do not think the argument has yet made clear its crucial claim. It might seem as if this freedom of choice, which is held to be essential for morality, was just a matter of 'doing this' rather than 'doing that' – visiting a sick friend rather than taking a country walk. But after this kind of fashion we might say of the ball rolling on the bagatelle table, that it did this

[1] It is described much more thoroughly and in far greater detail in C. D. Broad's Inaugural Lecture: *Determinism, Indeterminism and Libertarianism*, Cambridge, 1934, pp. 27-34.

rather than that, it scored 50 instead of 100, that it moved so as to actualise one of a number of possibilities. But plainly the moralist would not agree that the ball had the 'freedom' which belonged to a person when he responds dutifully to do one action rather than the other. What the moralist is contending for is not merely the possibility of alternatives. He is concerned to claim something about the way one of these alternatives is realised. He is saying that if we are to have responsible behaviour, then that particular one of the alternatives which we choose to do must be actualised by something very special, by what in fact he calls a 'free decision'. In short, to do my duty does not only imply that there was some kind of alternative to it: 'obligability' does not only imply 'substitutability'[1]; it implies also that I did what I did *in a certain sort of way*. Moralists claim that a 'free choice' or a 'responsible decision' contains something extra, besides that kind of actualising of one alternative rather than another which might characterise the movement of a bagatelle ball.

What now is this something extra? Here we approach the position sometimes called Libertarianism. According to this view, when a free choice actualises one alternative rather than another, there is something very special going on. What we do is being done in a special kind of way. What special sort of way? Libertarians will tell us, for example, that 'our timeless self opts for that alternative', or they will say that 'we are determined by the Moral Law to select that alternative'. Now, as C. D. Broad[2] points out with regard to the first possibility, it is questionable whether it is even intelligible, let alone true or false. Can we speak of a timeless self acting? Can something which is 'timeless' be the subject of a temporal verb? With regard to the second possibility, what can be meant by the Moral Law determining anything? Only belief in the moral law can determine this, that and the other. But belief, it would be said, is no more than a psychological event, and we seem to be back in complete determinism again.

[1] See C. D. Broad's Inaugural Lecture, pp. 6-7.
[2] On these points see C. D. Broad, *op. cit.*, pp. 42-47.

In short, while Libertarianism makes some attempt to say what is peculiar about, or extra in, a responsible decision, it does so in such a way as makes its case either unintelligibly confused, or self-defeating. But our conclusion need not be quite so negative. For the various expressions of Libertarianism (however pathetic) amount to a claim that what is extra in a moral decision (i) in some way or another is more than spatio-temporal events, and (ii) has something or other to do with our sense of obligation.

These claims do not fall simply because Libertarianism has not discovered a respectable language in which to express them. For the rest of this chapter, then, I propose to make somewhat clearer this peculiarity of moral decision on which the moralist insists, and on which the Libertarian insists though he talks of it so ill-advisedly – the claim that such a decision is 'more than' the 'observables'[1] it displays. We shall reserve for Chapter II a discussion of the connection between 'free will' and 'obligation'.

We have now seen how the scientist and the moralist would develop their respective approaches, the two approaches whose diversity made discussions of predictability fruitless, and whose conflicting claims give rise to the 'problem' of free will:

(*a*) On the one hand there is the claim that human behaviour, decisions included, is wholly reducible to what science talks about; that it can be satisfactorily treated without residue in terms of language appropriate to 'observables' or 'objects'.

(*b*) On the other hand there is the claim that there are certain decision-situations where, for example, we elect to do our duty, where the situation cannot be exhaustively described in perceptual terms.

We shall only solve the 'problem' of free will if we can support one of these claims to the exclusion of the other. To help us to do this, let us look at some typical cases of decision.

(*a*) Jim is a rather hen-pecked husband who loves to fly his pigeons, and one Bank Holiday there is a most exciting pigeon race being held in the neighbourhood. But we find him instead

[1] See p. 19.

on the front at New Brighton with his wife and children. 'I am surprised to see you here Jim', we say. 'Oh,' says his wife, 'He decided to come to New Brighton after all.' We look at Jim. Did he? We picture the various cause-factors in a discussion which, we may easily imagine, was mostly one-sided, and at the end of which Jim says, 'Yes, let's go to New Brighton.' There is no reason to suppose that with sufficient ability someone might not be able to tell a compelling causal story culminating in Jim's crucial remark. But to answer the question whether Jim *decided*, in the sense which both interests the moralist and is also connected with the problem of free will, it is not a matter of whether his words were or were not completely determined by antecedent cause-factors. The question is: Did Jim give his words his personal backing or not? Suppose Jim winks. It may be ambiguous. It may be what we would call the vanquished wink. This would imply, 'I have been subject again to external pressures, and yielded. I did not behave "like a man".' There may, on the other hand, be the victorious wink, which would imply, 'She thinks she won, but actually I did it freely.' But either way – vanquished or victor – the wink witnesses to two senses of decision. In one case the 'decision' had Jim's personal backing, and in the other case it had not. Further, only Jim can know. There need not be any difference in the cause-factors, in the 'observables'.

(*b*) For a second example, let us consider the Duke of Newcastle (was it not?) who dreamed he was making a speech in the House of Lords, and awoke to find that he was. Let us suppose that there was continuity in the speech, as well there might be. It could be as woolly and inconsequential afterwards, as it was before. True, there would be a distinctive change in the causal field at a particular point. One kind of more or less stable pattern would give way to another. That would be the distinction a scientist would draw between 'sleeping' and 'waking'. But suppose at the moment of waking the Duke decided to give his words henceforward *his personal backing*. Once again, only he would know. The causal pattern could be exactly the same in both cases. The difference would be that while all of it could be described homogeneously as 'He is speaking' or 'The noble lord is speaking', only part of it could be accurately described by the Duke as 'I am speaking'. The suggestion is, therefore, that what is significant about a personal backing, about the kind of decision on which the doctrine of free will concentrates, is something denoted by the word 'I' for each of us, and which is lost to such object words and phrases as 'He' or 'The noble duke'.

(*c*) Again, consider our activity in general, and in particular let us compare what is described as 'I'm running', said to myself, with what is described as 'He's running', said by another person about me. Of these two circumstances the spatio-temporal factors might be quite identical. But what the first case concerns more than these spatio-temporal features becomes evident when we reflect that it would be quite possible for me to say in such a case that nevertheless I 'couldn't help it', that I was running 'against my will', *and further*, this might be true where everything about my behaviour which was accessible to observation and inspection was identical with that on the other occasion where in fact I could help running and was actively willing to run. Once again, my personal backing, whether given or withheld, is something which a description in terms of 'objects' does not settle. Admittedly there will normally be easy criteria at hand to distinguish 'He's running because he can't help it' and 'He's running willingly'. But my argument is that there are some cases where only the runner himself can settle which of these assertions is true.

The point can perhaps be seen better if we consider the case of a professional runner whose movements and possibilities can be reliably predicted by trainers and others 'in the know'. And then one day, he astounds everybody. All the public features of the case would compel anyone to conclude that the man could not possibly still be running. For instance, we may have had from the start good reason to believe that today, because of some indisposition, the runner could not possibly be expected

23

to put up his usual performance. Yet there he goes, round and round the track – confounding each and every critic. It is in such a case that we talk of 'will-power', suggesting by this phrase that there is something about the man himself, and the effort he puts forth, which is quite inaccessible to spatio-temporal calculation. We say the same when in some serious illness, a specialist does not see how, from a medical point of view, the patient can continue to live; yet the day after, he is still alive and smiling. 'He must have tremendous will-power', we comment. The original medical judgment may or may not have been justified, but the fact that it is made on the one hand and thereafter supplemented by the other expression, shows that we all reckon with, and allow for, a certain human decisive activity which cannot be netted in that language of 'objects' and 'observables' which is, for example, the currency of medicine.[1]

The fact that decisive activity goes beyond and eludes 'object' language can be further illustrated by the example of a lecturer who is (say) giving his lecture for the five hundredth time. While 'He is lecturing' may be true of the whole hour, it may happen that at no point in that hour could the lecturer say of himself 'I'm lecturing', for at no time would he be giving a personal backing to his words. At no time would he be exercising 'decisive activity'. Even so, the object stories might still be identical with those to be told when the lecture was being given with due deliberation on the first occasion.

[1] In a note on a Coroner's inquest in *The Times* of May 6, 1958, *The Times* Medical Correspondent wrote: ' . . . there can be little doubt that the absence of the "will to live" can lead to a death for which, in our present state of knowledge, it is impossible to find a physical cause. . . . Conversely, every experienced doctor knows that the "will to live" is one of the most potent factors in ensuring recovery from a serious illness or operation. The close interrelationship of mind and body which was neglected with the advent of so-called "scientific medicine" at the turn of the century, is now accepted as one of the major challenges to the medical profession.'
While the Correspondent leaves the matter ultimately ambiguous by his use of the phrase 'in our present state of knowledge', the interest for our purpose is that when something occurs for which the language of 'scientific medicine' is not adequate, the phenomena are most naturally talked of in terms of 'the will' – 'the will to live'.

Again, there is the well-known story[1] of the man at the Army medical inspection who was being subjected to a rigorous examination which had been conducted in a thoroughly impersonal manner. Towards the end he was given the command, 'Clench your teeth', whereupon he removed them, handed them to the doctor, and said, 'Here, clench them yourself.' We might embroider the story. Suppose that doctor and soldier were 'as alike as two peas', even to having identical dentures; and that on hearing the command, the soldier removed the teeth, passed them to the doctor who, fitting them into his own identical mouth, thereupon clenched them. 'Clenching the teeth' would, for doctor and soldier be, in terms of 'objects', identical occurrences: but they would differ in so far as there was a difference in decisive activity, a difference which doctor and soldier would know for himself when the teeth happened to be in his mouth, but at no other time. Short of this decisive activity 'clenching the teeth' describes something which doctor and soldier could know equally well, no matter whose mouth held the teeth.

(d) Yet another example. The perfect actor reaches the peak of his success when he makes us believe that he is in fact the person whose part he is acting. The actor's public behaviour and appearance may be so similar to that of the person he is impersonating, and his performance so skilful that when, for example, a schoolboy is asked 'Who was Henry VIII?' he can answer unashamedly 'Charles Laughton'. But there are two persons who would know for certain who was who: Henry VIII and Charles Laughton respectively. Neither would ever be in the position of wondering whether after all he was himself or the other man. So it is that while 'I' stands in part for my public behaviour to which everyone has equal access, behaviour which in certain cases may be, as near as makes no matter, identical with the behaviour of someone else, 'I' also stands for something more, and Charles Laughton would know that 'something more' when he 'decided of his own free will' to take the part of Henry VIII.

[1] For myself, I am indebted to Miss G. E. M. Anscombe for it.

So the claim of free will is the claim that at a moment of 'free' decision there occurs a situation not restricted to the spatio-temporal events it contains – those events which are the 'objects' in terms of which everyone, including me, will describe it afterwards. We have argued that this claim can be justified by reflecting on such ordinary language as (*pace* some contemporary philosophers) does justice to the complexity of ordinary situations. We make a 'free' decision when we are not just this or that behaviour pattern, but when we are 'men', when each of us is distinctively 'I'. At such moments of decision, when all of us characteristically use of ourselves the word 'I', this word covers more than all language about objects or all scientific language talks about. The wink on the Promenade at New Brighton differs significantly from a fall of the lid to clean the eye, though this in part it is. The claim for free will is, then, that in a moment of decision there is disclosed the 'transcendent' character of a man's personality. It is in making such a decision that he realises he is not limited to the objective behaviour he displays to a scientific observer. Undoubtedly, each one of us is a veritable biochemical playground for fats, proteins and carbohydrates; we may well agree, too, that very much of what we do is economically conditioned. Further, all of us exhibit in profusion instincts, emotions, reflexes, complexes and inhibitions, and we have an unconscious which is always liable to pop up to the threshold. We can all readily recognise the point of a psychologist's mythology. But all that granted, the believer in free will holds that in a certain kind of decisive action a man realises himself as something more than language or all of these stories – be they of biochemistry, economics, psychology, and so on – talk about. In our second chapter we shall look further at these significant cases of decisive action.

Meanwhile we may reflect that the best 'arguments' for free will are the kinds of situation our recent examples[1] have been meant to evoke and recapture.

[1] See pp. 21-25.

II

FREEDOM: OBLIGATION

WE BEGAN our discussion of freedom by looking at the arguments about predictability and unpredictability. We saw, on the one hand, that if we begin by assuming that human behaviour is predictable, we can always continue our argument against any opposition by appealing to cause-factors which have been overlooked. On the other hand, if we begin by arguing that human behaviour is unpredictable, we can always continue our argument against any opposition by appealing to more and more specific features of the particular behaviour in question. But from this apparently profitless and unending discussion and as lying behind it, there emerge two views. One of these regards human behaviour as a complex pattern of spatio-temporal events and no more. The other view holds that there are certain cases of distinctively human behaviour where no story about spatio-temporal events or 'objects' – however complex – will be adequate. Now when the problem of free will is said to be one of science *versus* morality, these are the background presuppositions which broadly speaking characterise science and morality respectively. But further discussion of these two approaches revealed that the crucial question for free will centred on decisions: which of these two presuppositions does most justice to characteristic occasions of decision? So we took some examples designed to show that, quite apart from such parts of a man's behaviour as can be the topic of scientific investigation, and which might at a particular time show the actualisation of one possibility rather than of another

– something which might be called 'impersonal decision' – quite apart from all this, there is the possibility of such public behaviour having what we called a man's 'personal backing'. If it had such backing there was then a characteristically 'personal decision' which would not be reducible to public behaviour any more than 'I'm running' (said by me) described a situation wholly identical with 'he's running' (said by you at the same time). My behaviour, to me, when deliberate or decisive, is 'objects' *and more*. Thus, the claim of free will is the claim that there are certain decision-situations not restricted to those 'objects' in terms of which everybody besides me describes them now, and everybody, including me, describes them afterwards. The phrase 'acts of will', as describing situations of characteristically personal decision which are not reducible to the spatio-temporal 'objects' they contain, cannot therefore, without logical confusion, be talked of as if it were no more than a spatio-temporal event. It rather describes that ontological peculiar which is decisive action.

What I wish to do in the present chapter is to link this discussion about decision with the other theme involved in the problem of free will – that of duty or obligation. What is involved in the claim that to do my duty I must be free? How do we develop a connection between freedom (as we have interpreted it) and morality?

To answer this question let us begin by looking at some further cases of decision. These cases of decision we shall consider not so much for the light they throw on the character of decision as such – that has been our earlier concern. Our hope is that they will rather illuminate the connection between free will and obligation.

The first example has a rather grim beginning. Suppose there has been a road accident – we hear in quick succession a screeching of brakes, a crashing of metal against metal, screams and groans, and we leap up to see dismembered bodies, patches of blood and so on.

Now, from a strictly scientific standpoint here is a situation which might be regarded in some ways as a large-scale version of the grinding of meat in an inefficient mincer turned by a vile-tempered butcher: here again are noises metallic and human preceding a cutting up of flesh and dispersal of blood. In the kind of terms appropriate to mincing and human psychology, the scene might be given a scientific description, a description wholly in terms of 'objects'.

Now suppose that a doctor happens to live only a few yards from the scene. He hears the noise and rushes out. Even so, what he does, *need* not be regarded as anything more than an appropriate reaction to stimuli. All the habits of behaviour the doctor once learnt in laboratory and hospital have come into their own, and whatever he does might be done with all the efficiency of a trained automaton. There need not, in other words, be anything moral about the situation. A set of complex machines elaborately constructed might do the job equally well, just as the photo-electric burglar alarm can be a substitute for the work of a night watchman. Instead of the man's shout, the bell rings. Similarly, in an accident area there might be machines which on the reception of noise of a certain intensity, disinfected the air, dispersed tranquillisers to the noise *foci*, provided stimulants, hot drinks and so on. Altogether there might be a world braver and newer than even Huxley's *Brave New World*. Here then is the doctor reacting to stimuli. Nor need such a story finish at this point.

Suppose at the time of the accident the doctor was reading the *British Medical Journal* with the efficiency due to his profession, or playing bridge with the efficiency due to his friends. He might still, unmoved, continue to do the one or the other, or he might leave the one or the other to go to the scene of the crash. But we need not say he 'decided' to go to the crash. He might go (we would say) quite 'automatically'. It might still be a matter of training, responsibility, habit, so that the greatest force won. Once again, it would only be reaction to stimuli, but a much more complex reaction appropriate to the greater range and variety of stimuli. Here would be 'impersonal decision', as we have called it, if we wanted to talk about 'decision' at all. It would be the doing of one thing rather than another. A scientific account of the 'decision' in terms of 'objects' would be wholly adequate.

But now the story can change. The doctor, on hearing the accident, might say he was 'obliged' (however unfortunate it might seem) to leave the *British Medical Journal* or his friends. He might start to talk of a 'duty to humanity', of a 'challenge' to which he must respond. To any efficient reaction there would now be added his personal backing. He would exercise free will and responsible decision. The suggestion is that such free and personal decision occurs when there is a challenge and a claim which issues from the 'objects' but is not restricted to them, to which challenge and claim the free decision is a response. A free decision is neither, on the one hand, merely a reaction to stimuli; nor on the other hand is it – what the reader may have supposed so far – some altogether circumscribed, independent, isolated going-on which is all my own. A free decision is a personal response – something certainly my very own – but it is a response to a discerned obligation which exceeds 'observables'.

For our second example let us recall the story of the Good Samaritan.[1] Its theme is familiar. A man is robbed on the road between Jerusalem and Jericho and left half dead, whereupon three travellers come to the scene.

The first, a priest, at once passes by on the other side. Engaged in Temple duties and responsible for its worship, he must not violate the ceremonial law and become unclean. His behaviour pattern in fact follows exactly the prescriptions of the priestly law. He goes on. There is, we might remark, no deflection whatever of the galvanometer. The situation is all very impersonal. 'The priest', as the 'official', moves through his prescribed behaviour patterns, and we speak of him as 'inhuman' and 'callous', as hard and impersonal as a piece of bone.

Then comes the Levite, whom we may describe as a subordinate Temple official, concerned very much with proprieties

[1] Luke 10.30-35.

of one kind and another. For instance, the Levite (I understand) looked after the transport of the Tabernacle and its furniture; sometimes he collected tithe, and on occasions he kept the City Gate on the Sabbath to see that no merchandise made its way into the city on that day. In short, he had a behaviour pattern somewhat wider than that of the priest, and he had also that fussy inquisitiveness which often belongs to vergers or deputy registrars. It was as though, in his case, the galvanometer needle quivered just a little. But in the end he, too, had no prescribed rule for dealing with the situation, and so 'decided' to pass on, as we may speak of the bagatelle ball 'deciding' to go in this hole rather than that. Once again the situation is very impersonal, very 'inhuman'. Neither the priest nor the Levite is a 'man' any more than the hen-pecked husband at New Brighton. Physiologically, sociologically, and so on, of course they are all men; but in that sense which, while it takes account of all such features, goes beyond them as well, they are not.

So to the Samaritan. He, too, had a rule which could have regulated his behaviour. Since the Jews had no dealings with the Samaritans he could easily have 'decided' to pass on like the others. His external behaviour might have been such that it sheered away from the wounded man rather than centred around him. But in this case more than rule or law is involved; more than public and external behaviour. It is not that 'Samaritan' meets 'Jew', but that 'man' meets 'man', and we see more clearly what duty to humanity involves. Directly the Samaritan sees the wounded man, forthwith, as the aorist form of the verb emphasises,[1] he is moved, provoked to action. It is not now a reaction determined by external stimuli. Rather is he stirred by something called 'compassion'. The Samaritan is moved 'inwardly' by the challenge of the suffering man. Bandage, oil, wine, beast, time, money, and more – whatever more is wanted – will be given as an expression of this compassion. So the Samaritan's response – as befits the challenge – exceeds any specific determination. He has responded to a moral obligation.

[1] Luke 10.33 (ἐσπλαγχνίσθη).

He has been a man, not an 'official', and the wounded man on the road has not been merely a 'Jew' or (as for the priest and Levite) something 'unclean' according to the Law, but someone who excited a challenge which no such 'object' language could contain. A moral obligation cannot be netted in the language of observables whether this be civil or ceremonial law.

For a third example, consider the efficient booking clerk. We might say that with each traveller he makes a 'decision'. Following each request from beyond the grille, a specific behaviour pattern occurs. He hears the name, takes the money, punches the ticket, bangs down the change. So far there is nothing in his behaviour, nothing about his 'decision' which suggests anything more than external spatio-temporal events. An efficient machine could do the job as well, and in many cases (we might reflect) even better.

But suppose he looks through the grille one day and the face he sees is of a man who is 'wanted'. Here is the man associated with some murder – we may even suppose it concerned the booking clerk's own son. The situation now comes alive. It is no longer a case of a grille and a passenger's face, but there is a moment of 'decision' of a kind that has not been known in the booking office for years. This decision which the clerk takes, the decision to catch the man, is certainly free and personal. But it is also 'responsible', for it is a response to a challenge which is a moral challenge, a challenge which while it issues from certain external events is not merely the challenge of those events being just as they are, there. Neither does what is 'more' about the moral challenge just mean that, in a causal sort of way, this face beyond the grille was in such and such circumstances associated with the death of the clerk's son, who was of course causally associated by procreation with the booking clerk, and so on. All that is, naturally, true, and even by itself it admittedly makes the decision-situation different from one which merely concerns any old traveller buying any old ticket. But the claim would be that no such description of external events, however complex and far-reaching, would tell the whole truth about the challenge which is recognised at the moment the 'free' and 'personal' decision is made. What happens at that moment exceeds any description of external 'objects' however complex. And what (the reader may ask) is our justification for saying that? The answer is that the whole point of the stories we have been telling lies in their ability to recapture for the reader that 'moment' at which the situation takes on 'depth', becoming observables *and more*. The story has been told precisely in the hope that the reader will then 'see' for himself what is characteristically different about a moral obligation, and what is meant by saying that such an obligation is more than the objects or observables it contains.

These three examples, then, have suggested that a 'free' decision is rightly seen as a response, and as a response to a challenge of a peculiar kind. While a 'plain' or 'impersonal' or 'natural' decision may be causally connected with and determined by 'objects' alone, a 'free' decision – a decision which is backed personally – is a response to 'objects' and more. It is this 'transcendent' reference which makes the challenge moral: to be aware of such a challenge is to recognise a moral obligation. Further, it is in involving such a recognition and in being such a response, that a free decision can be rightly called 'responsible'.

To make the character of this obligation and challenge plainer, let us now continue our examples with some which also examine more closely this difference between making a plain and a responsible decision, the difference we have expressed earlier as one between making a personal and an impersonal decision.[1]

Let us consider, first, two examples of plain decisions. Suppose someone says, 'I have decided that the Principle of Archimedes is credible', and we ask, 'Why?' The answer that would be given might go something like this. Presented with a particular sequence of 'objects' – or observables – a cylinder and piston in air; the piston in water; and lastly the piston in water with also the empty cylinder filled with water – I watch the scales of the balance change from being horizontal, first

[1] See e.g. pp. 28 and 30.

dropping on the weights side, and then returning to the horizontal again. When all that happens, I then say that a body (like this piston) when immersed in water, suffers an up-thrust equal to the weight of water displaced. Here is something – the Principle of Archimedes – which I read off from the observations. Here is a language which has generalised from the 'objects' of this particular experiment. My 'decision' that the Principle of Archimedes is credible, means no more than that the assertion we made above is appropriately attached to this particular sequence of objects. We read off the Principle from the observations just as we might easily generalise about those men who are no more than units in an impersonal army group.

For the second example of a 'plain' decision let us consider someone who says in Birkenhead, 'To reach Oswestry I have decided to travel via Chester and Ruabon rather than by Runcorn and Crewe.' We then ask, 'Why?' It might be that, faced with one alternative rather more complex than the other, our prospective passenger has pursued the 'line of least resistance'. He may have behaved exactly like a particle in a physics book on the properties of matter. Or it might be that what he might see on the one route, or might smell on the other, determined his decision. But if his answers are such as these, his decision would be quite 'impersonal'.

In contrast to this let us now look at decisions which, while they may begin by appearing to be 'plain' and may even in certain cases remain 'plain', can nevertheless be more than this, whereupon they would be said to be 'responsible'. Suppose someone says, 'I have decided that this thesis merits a D.Phil.', and we ask why. A possible answer might start something like this: 'Well, it is just about under 100,000 words, has a 20-page bibliography; the candidate has read all the relevant books; there are no major blunders, and so on – ought he not to get the degree – at least for hard work, *laboris causa* if not *honoris causa*?' Someone might say 'Yes' and thus register a 'plain' decision; but another would comment, 'I am not interested in features of that sort, as such; it rather sounds as though you think he deserves the degree because of the weight of paper he has submitted. What I am concerned about is the "quality" or "standard" of the thesis – something which is not tied rigorously to such characteristics as you have given us – words, bibliography, typography, and so on – though these are relevant.' What now is different about the decision someone makes when he decides to award a D.Phil. on 'quality'?

Or again, it is no doubt fairly easy to draw up a class list in elementary mathematics where there is only one prescribed method and answer to each question. But how do we decide to put someone in Class I – or for that matter in any class – when, whether it be mathematics or any other subject, there are no prescribed answers? In such cases we speak of the man's proofs being 'neat' and his work being very 'impressive', or the reverse. So our judgment, while being based on the 'facts', i.e. what can be talked about in terms of the number of words, the length of the bibliography, and so on, nevertheless goes beyond these facts, and we speak of the decision being 'responsible'. Our decision is a response to that claim of the work which we call its 'impressive quality'. I am not saying, of course, that of necessity every responsible decision is, in virtue of being responsible, inevitably correct. That is another story. What justifies the decision is something different from what makes it responsible. All I am contending now is that a *responsible* decision, where we respon1 to 'objects' and more, differs significantly from a *plain* decision which is causally related only to such 'objects' as words and typography.

To take a second example let us consider the case of someone who says to us, 'I have decided to be a doctor', and again we ask, 'Why?' If one kind of answer is given it will be evident that his 'decision' has been plain and impersonal. This kind of answer would run something like the following: 'My friends tell me that there is good money to be found under the National Health Service. Nor is there much difficulty these days in getting temperatures down with anti-biotics and the like. Further, any puzzles can always be referred to consultants at hospitals, and so on. Finally, the British Medical Association will always be ready to dissuade people from being over-troublesome in epidemics.' In this case we might well say that the decision to be a doctor was 'inhuman', and anyone who decided to be a doctor with *no more than* such considerations in mind need not be surprised if, when he walks the ward, he hears it said of him, 'There comes that old battle-axe again.' The impersonal description and model will be surprisingly apt.

Supposing, however, someone says, 'I have reckoned with all that, but it is not the whole story. I feel "called" to be a doctor. To me it is a genuine "vocation".' Then once again the decision becomes responsible – it is regarded as a 'response' to a 'call'. That it was 'responsible' might be verified when, for example, the second doctor walks in the ward, for, if the doctor has a genuine 'vocation' we can be sure that the patients will not think it appropriate to use 'battle-axe' language about the situation.

Finally, suppose someone says, 'I have decided to be married.' Once again we ask, 'Why?' The reply may be, 'Oh, it is because I cannot keep the bachelor-girl flat going any longer', or, if our conversation is with a male, 'Because I cannot afford to pay so much for housekeepers.' Or, we may be told, 'Well, old man, it is because I want to save psychiatrists' bills in later years.' With all such answers we know that the kind of decision that 'deciding to be married' has been, is no more than a 'plain' decision.

But, as we know, there are other situations in which people use such phrases as 'falling in love', whose logic is obviously extremely odd, for, as far as can be seen, people have fallen into nothing, but are indeed as alert and brisk as ever they were, and even brisker. Further, if someone says, 'I have decided to be married because I am devoted to the person who is to be my wife' (or husband, as the case may be), then it is considered appropriate to express this devotion in phrases such as 'for better for worse, for richer for poorer, in sickness and in health'. In short, the devotion will stand whatever the empirical considerations, whether the circumstances be black or white, positive or negative. It is true of course that some may say that these phrases describe no more than an empirically variegated devotion. But I suggest that they are meant to advertise and insist on the fact that the devotion which is being talked about, while expressing itself in various observable directions, is something that cannot be entirely cashed in terms of those observational features alone. The phrases 'for better for worse, for richer for poorer, in sickness and in health' tell of a devotion which is non-falsifiable, which can never be caught out, which can contain within itself this or that particular circumstance. But this does not mean that it is disingenuously vacuous and irrelevant. For something very significant and far-reaching can happen to it. It can disappear altogether, when those who were once devoted will have so changed as to be 'converted' – converted into infidelity. Nothing will be the same again.

All these examples, then, make two points.

1. Though this was not the particular reason for introducing them, they emphasise and, I hope, make clearer the kind of decision for which the doctrine of free will contends; what we called earlier an impersonal and later a 'responsible' decision, a decision which is more than a 'plain' decision, a decision which is rightly called 'free' because it is free from the total restraint of causal language. The public behaviour pattern before and after any such decision may be determined. There may or may not be a certain discontinuity in the behaviour pattern at a particular boundary, but if there is, such discontinuity may be admittedly *part* of what we mean by decision, and *all* of what we mean by a plain decision.

2. But the particular purpose, for which the examples were specially introduced, was to emphasise that the kind of decision which typifies free will must be seen as a response to a challenge that, like the decision, is spatio-temporal, but also more than spatio-temporal, a challenge which is observables and more.

At last the full range of the free will claim makes itself evident. The situation claimed by the doctrine of free will concerns:

subjectively a characteristic sort of decision in which a person transcends his public behaviour, acts more than 'officially'; and this as a response to what is *objectively* a challenge which equally transcends public terms, a challenge we call 'duty' or 'obligation'.

Let us notice three corollaries to this view.

1. *Free Will and Causation*

We can now see how misleading it is, because logically inappropriate, to try to discuss free will in a causal context.

We have been at pains to agree that in *one* sort of decision nothing more need be said beyond saying that my behaviour is causally determined by some sort of objects. The cause-effect relationship which specifies a scientific connectedness, may, in *some* cases of behaviour, be entirely appropriate. Such cases would be that of the efficient doctor or booking clerk, the official priest or Levite, the elementary physicist, or the traveller to Oswestry who took the line of least resistance.

But the determination of my will, the determination of my decision when there is free will, is no causal determination. It is a peculiar kind of response to a peculiar kind of challenge.

Let us recall the claim of Libertarianism. When the Libertarian says, 'My behaviour is determined by the Moral Law', this may mean (what for instance Dr C. D. Broad was prepared to take it to mean), 'My behaviour, which is in principle wholly public, follows my belief in the Moral Law.' That is a causal assertion, and it would be quite compatible with complete determinism of a scientific sort, which *inter alia* extended throughout physiology and psychology. But the claim of Libertarianism may mean, and has generally meant, something other than this, though not something necessarily incompatible with it. It has then been a claim that my total behaviour is a decisive response to the challenge, itself transcending objects, which the phrase 'Moral Law' (we ourselves may think not too satisfactorily) labels. In short, the logic of 'My action is determined by the Moral Law' is much more like 'I am responding to his love and affection' than it is like 'I am reacting to his stimuli and his treatment.'

2. *Obligation and God*

In this second corollary let us approach a traditional difficulty about God's will and Duty, by first developing further the view of obligations which lies behind our treatment of free will.

(*a*) Very naturally the obligations we most readily recognise are those which centre around other people, who are then more than 'official'. There is the bus conductor, whose action week in, week out, may be no more than that of any 'official' to me as a 'passenger'. But one day we see him, not as a conductor, but as a man. Something of his home, his family, his working hours, his wages, has come to our knowledge. Arising from this wider context, but inevitably going beyond it, is a moral challenge, and we speak of having a 'social conscience' about him. Our response to the conductor, while having still its customary public expression, is thus free as it has not been free before. It is not now merely the response of a 'passenger'.

(*b*) But someone may say, 'I still do not see what sort of thing this moral challenge is – this which arises out of but goes beyond a certain empirical pattern.' To such a complaint we may reply as follows: Let us notice that we can all give to some situations a challenge of this logically peculiar kind by incorporating them in a promise. We ourselves in this way can create a moral challenge. Any of my promises are declarations by myself that I have given a moral challenge to such and such circumstances which, without the promise, would not normally express such a challenge at all. For instance, I say to my small son, 'You will have the new Dinky toy next month.' Or again, we promise our boy, 'I will show you Archimedes' Principle tomorrow', or 'We will go to Oswestry next year.' In these ways our promise makes situations which would be otherwise quite neutral, duty bearing. The shop window containing next month the new Dinky toy on its stand, is not merely a matter of what's seen. By my promise, there belongs to it for me a moral challenge.

Similarly, it is no longer a matter of reading off Archimedes' Principle. To do this in response to a promise is to see the scientific pattern as the bearer and expression of a moral challenge which goes beyond it. Likewise, a trip to Oswestry is no mere behaviour according to a line of least resistance. We now do it as a duty.

(*c*) Such is what we mean by recognising particular obligations. Now let us develop the picture somewhat by noticing that sometimes these particular obligations usefully combine, while at other times they are somewhat distressingly in conflict. We may buy a new Dinky toy on our trip to Oswestry and so fulfil both promises, both obligations, at the same time. But at other times obligations conflict. What we do then, and by means of argument and discussion, is further enumerate relevant 'objects', hoping that as the pattern becomes more and more detailed there will emerge my particular duty on that particular occasion. This would then be the particular version, suited to those particular circumstances, of that Duty which would reconcile all partial duties, the Duty which would emerge from what W. D. Ross[1] called '*prima facie* duties'. Let us see by an example how all this works. Let us allow for the sake of illustration, that a man has three duties: a duty to his family, a duty to Society, and a duty to tell the truth, especially if his profession involves public speaking. Here are *prima facie* obligations that grow out of what are in the first instance fairly restricted empirical areas. For instance, a duty to his family will arise from, even if it goes beyond, the picture he has of them sitting with him around the dining-room table, playing in the garden and so on. His duty to Society will arise from the picture he has of various folk in very different towns, in very different countries. His duty to tell the truth will arise from sentences and documents that he is concerned to study and assess. Suppose now, as a concrete case, we have a married philosopher aspiring to become a Member of Parliament. Let him be Mr Cumnor Hurst. Now very often Mr Cumnor Hurst's duties may conflict.

[1] *The Right and the Good*, Oxford, 1930, pp. 18-36.

In his desire to be an M.P. and fulfil his duties to Society, he may have to make speeches which compromise his duty to truth; if in his duty to truth he is strenuously exerting himself at a philosophical Dinner, he may be neglecting his family who are having sardines in the kitchen at home. But on some occasion all the *prima facie* obligations may happily combine. To see this in a certain instance we must particularise. The picture of the family will have to be given a wider setting than the home; his philosophical exertions will have to be displayed to other than his immediate colleagues; his duty to Society must be given a broader expression than the intention to become an M.P. Whereupon he may see it as his Duty to accept an invitation to talk to a mixed youth group at Little Snoring, where his wife and family can accompany him and join in the refreshments. As the picture is developed with its various details, the particular obligations which each restricted picture served to preserve and express, coalesce into one, and a pattern of behaviour is prescribed which is a translation into particular circumstances of the Duty whose challenge Mr Cumnor Hurst would always wish to discern, and to which he would always wish to respond, the Duty which still transcends any and all behaviour patterns. Mr Cumnor Hurst does not go to Little Snoring simply because it is a cheap supper for the family, or because free-for-all travelling expenses are paid, or because he is an extrovert. His visit is not determined by his desire for the publicity which the *Snoring and Bedlam Gazette* will most certainly supply. If he went simply for any and all of these reasons, he would not go as a response to Duty. To go as a response to Duty by no means implies that such points have been excluded from consideration, but it does imply that the decision was not causally determined by them. The decision was rather a response to the challenge which they and much else expressed, and which went beyond them all.

In an endeavour to do justice to this Duty which breaks in on us as something more than the observables we are scanning and enumerating, people have sometimes talked of Duty in a way that belittles all kinds of empirical calculation. They have spoken of 'Duty for duty's sake' (and for nothing else – least of all for free refreshments or newspaper publicity), or of Duty being 'independent of consequences' (whatever the *Snoring and Bedlam Gazette* does about the visit). But all this is a grossly misleading and impossibly exaggerated attempt to emphasise what is an important truth: viz. that when Duty breaks in on us, it is something not limited to the observable factors which are its translation in spatio-temporal terms. What makes Duty *characteristically* Duty is the *transcendent* setting that these terms are given. Mr Cumnor Hurst is not fulfilling his duty if he has been stimulated to visit Little Snoring *wholly* by economic and publicity considerations. 'Duty' or 'Absolute Value' is what challenges us 'objectively' when as a result of moral reflection there breaks in on us as something going beyond the 'objects', that which demands a unique personal response showing itself in certain particular behaviour in a given circumstance.

One more example: a passenger liner is sinking, and all the boats have been lowered. No more lifebelts are available, and there are still many passengers left on the ship and unprovided for. People are trying frantically but without much success, to break up chairs to which they may possibly cling. Everybody is working for himself and himself alone: the instinct of self-preservation dominates everyone's behaviour. Then a steward catches sight of a small child crying for his parents. In one way, here is just another noise on a ship full of men and women shouting and brawling and behaving like terror-stricken animals. But for the steward it is otherwise. He at once 'sees' his Duty. Here is an additional empirical feature – the cry of the child – which transforms the whole situation. At once the steward becomes a man again. He sits with the child, cares for him and comforts him. Eventually, both are drowned together, but without panic or struggle. A catalogue of the spatio-temporal features would not in the end be vastly different than it would have been whatever the steward had done. But the last ten minutes on the ship exemplified a challenge and a response which was characteristically dutiful, for both challenge and response transcended the empirical situation through which they were expressed.

When a humanist recognises, as many humanists would, this transcendence, he will speak of the moral significance – the absolute value – which the steward saw in a helpless bewildered child, and of the steward discerning a Duty to Humanity. A believer in God will speak of the steward seeing God in the little child – 'one of these little ones'[1] – of the steward doing God's will. The steward himself might well have reflected, 'It is God's will that I should comfort and look after this child', as others have often said, 'It's God's will that I should provide diligently for my family, work for social amelioration, tell the truth . . .' and so on. What now have we to say about these different interpretations offered to us by the humanist and the theist respectively? One interprets a situation in terms of 'Duty' and 'Absolute Value'; the other speaks of 'God' and God's will'. What is the relation between their differing interpretations?

To raise that question takes us at once to a recent controversy, in which Lord Russell and Professor Ayer were participants. The controversy centred around the claim that the existence of 'Absolute Values' does not at all necessitate belief in God, and has in fact no bearing on such a belief. Lord Russell,[2] like the humanist we have mentioned, admitted on the one hand that he was compelled to believe in absolute ethical values: 'I cann¯t believe that a dislike of wanton cruelty is merely a matter of taste, like a dislike of oysters.' Nevertheless, he added, 'I am in complete agreement with Professor Ayer in thinking that the question whether ethical values are absolute has no bearing whatever on the question of the existence of God.' Lord Russell would say that there is no relation whatever between the two interpretations which the humanist and the theist respectively gives us. But Professor Ayer[3] wished to go further and to urge

[1] Matt. 18.10.   [2] Letter to *The Observer*, Oct. 20, 1957.
[3] Letter to *The Observer*, Oct. 13, 1957.

that the humanist's interpretation excludes that of the theist. He argued that it is inconsistent to hold *both* that 'ethical values are absolute' *and* yet that they are 'validated by authority', even if the authority be that of God. Now what is the truth behind these contentions? What have we to say about the relationship between our sense of Duty and our belief in God?

Let us begin with Lord Russell's position. For him, the assertion 'Cruelty is always wrong' expresses an 'absolute value', though (if we may make a point which reveals the difficulty of expressing 'absolute values' in maxims) we may notice that Russell has to specify cruelty further as 'wanton cruelty'. He plainly has in mind, for example, such circumstances as the ruthless beating of children, or the evils of a Concentration Camp. What all this means, I suggest, is that, for Russell, stories of wanton cruelty evoke a situation transcending but including observables to whose challenge he responds by resisting cruelty or working for the destruction of whatever or whoever is cruel. Presented with 'wanton cruelty' Russell feels 'obliged' to oppose it; he discerns a Duty to eradicate it. Let us notice, for instance, how Russell emphasises that this response is not at all like his response to oysters, though he 'dislikes' cruelty and he also 'dislikes' oysters. But his 'dislike' of oysters is a 'dislike' which would plainly be no more than a complex spatio-temporal reaction in terms of taste, smell, 'feel' in the mouth and so on. Not that even this dislike would have anything 'purely subjective' about it. It would concern the oysters as much as it concerns Russell. But the cruelty situation differs from the oyster situation because while it centres around and expresses itself in spatio-temporal observables it also transcends such observables. In this way and for this reason (we would say) it presents Russell with a *moral* challenge. To such a challenge he then makes an appropriate moral response, in this case a resistance. It is (he would say) his 'Duty' to oppose cruelty. It is in relation to situations such as these – which include but are not limited to observable features – that the phrase 'absolute values' finds its justification and empirical anchorage. It is in such a situation that the phrase 'absolute values' is pegged down. For we recognise an 'absolute value' whenever we recognise that which challenges us in a moral situation, and recognise it as being more than what presents itself spatio-temporally. To go back again to Russell's example, 'cruelty is always wrong' expresses an 'absolute value' when there cluster round the maxim such stories of cruelty as evoke a situation which is distinctively different from the oyster situation in being not only what's seen, what's tasted ... and so on, but *more besides*, more than all such spatio-temporal presentations. The oyster-cruelty contrast thus takes its place with the other stories we have told – about the doctor, the Samaritan, the booking-clerk and so on[1] – and we have told all of them in order to bring out what is distinctive about a 'Duty' situation, what is distinctive about the challenge which obligation brings with it, what makes a situation moral. All these stories, however diverse, have one aim, viz. the evocation of a characteristic situation which transcends but includes observables, a situation which is not limited to what's seen ... etc. but which is all that and more besides. It is only by reference to such a situation that we can justify talk about 'absolute values'.

Let us admit, however, that nothing we have said so far of itself and by itself necessitates belief in God. Thus far Lord Russell is right, and Ayer is also right when he says that 'if cruelty is absolutely wrong, it would still be wrong even if, as Christians would say *per impossibile*, the superior being did not condemn it'.[2] So far there is complete agreement between us on conclusions, at any rate, though I do not pretend that there would be complete agreement about the arguments supporting them. Indeed, Russell himself admits that he is dissatisfied with his position. He has to agree with his reviewer that 'my ethics are unsatisfactory'[3] since he cannot 'meet the arguments against absolute values', nor yet agree with them. What I am suggesting is that arguments against 'absolute values' will never be satis-

[1] See pp. 28-33 above.   [2] Letter in *The Observer*, Oct. 13, 1957.
[3] Letter in *The Observer*, Oct. 20, 1957.

factorily met unless and until we give the phrase the empirical anchorage we have tried to give to it in this chapter. As long as 'absolute values' is given any other placing – for instance, supposing the phrase to be directly descriptive of some curious feature in an occult realm, so long will the attack on 'absolute values' thrive. The only reply to arguments against 'absolute values' is (I suggest) to evoke the kind of situation to which Russell implicitly appeals when he distinguishes his dislike of oysters from his dislike of cruelty, the latter being a discernment which goes beyond 'what's tasted and seen'. But to do this is to be moving in the direction of religious belief.[1] We are beginning to move from the humanist's to the theist's interpretation: which brings us back to the question of the difference between them. Suppose we all agree, as we can do, on the existence of 'absolute values', and even that belief in 'absolute values' does not of itself and by itself compel belief in God. Is it also true that belief in 'absolute values' has (as Russell believes) no bearing whatever on belief in God? Or, still worse, must a belief in God (as Ayer suggests) even compromise belief in 'absolute values'? Ayer says, for instance, 'There is . . . a logical inconsistency in maintaining . . . both that values are absolute and that they are validated by authority; and this inconsistency is not removed by supposing the authority to be divine.'[2] What do we say to these further contentions? Having clarified (as I hope) the concept of 'absolute values', how do we connect this with the concept of God?

Let us say at once that if the world contained nothing but obligations as instances of what we have called 'distinctive situations', if we were never aware at any time of any other brand of situations which are what's seen, what's tasted . . . and more besides, if *all* 'distinctive situations' arose in connection with morality, then we might well believe that some such phrase as 'Duty' or 'Absolute Values' was the only metaphysical

[1] See, for instance, my *Religious Language*, London, 1957, where I argue that what specially characterises a religious situation is such a discernment and an appropriate response.

[2] Letter in *The Observer*, Oct. 13, 1957.

phrase anyone need bother to have. There would hardly be any point in introducing as a further complication the word 'God'. Such phrases as 'Duty' or 'Absolute Values' might seem perfectly sufficient for specifying our 'ultimate' understanding of the universe in terms of our most significant insights. To do our Duty or to realise 'Absolute Values' would, as responses to such insight, exhaust our distinctive behaviour. But in fact the world contains much else than moral obligations, and the theist will now point out that we can tell many other stories, stories this time about non-moral factors of the universe, which lead to similar disclosures. There are the stories, for example, about causes, and existents, which are generated by such phrases as 'first cause' and 'necessary being'. These phrases, as I have shown elsewhere,[1] are to be regarded as qualified models which, acting as mnemonics, generate stories, stories about 'causes' or 'beings' or whatever 'exists', whose point and hope is to evoke disclosure situations similar to those which arise around obligations. While the stories might seem from one point of view a never-ending wild-goose chase after the 'first cause' or some 'necessary being', from another point of view they carry with them a never-ending possibility that at some point or other as the causal survey grows ever more compulsive, or the enumeration of existents ever more far-reaching, a discernment may break in on us, and a typically religious response be made. Then in fact we know what a 'distinctive situation' is, and how it can be reached by a non-moral route.

In short, there are available, for evoking such distinctive situations, all those stories that are described by the traditional title of the non-moral arguments for the existence of God. By these stories, the believer claims that distinctive disclosure situations can be evoked similar to those which occur when we are aware of obligations or sense our Duty.

Let us acknowledge, then, that disclosure situations can be evoked by the most diverse stories. The next step in the argu-

[1] See *Religious Language*, esp. Ch. II. In the present book somewhat more detailed examples are given on pp. 57 and 92.

ment is to recognise that it is in regard to what is evoked *subjectively* in all these disclosures that the word 'I' gains its appropriate logical placing. For I am never more 'myself' than in such a distinctive situation[1] – when, for instance, I make a free decision to respond to an obligation. If then 'I' is an appropriate label for all the disclosure situations on the subjective side, why should we not introduce the word 'God' as a sort of objective counterpart to 'I'? The basic justification for the word 'God', then, is that in talking about the universe, in reckoning with distinctive situations, we find that we need to talk of more than Duty and Absolute Value. 'God' thus takes its place with the various words and phrases which one by one specify what is distinctively objective about this or that disclosure-situation: 'Duty', 'Absolute Value', 'First Cause', 'Necessary Being', and so on.

The next move in the argument comes when we ask, somewhat naturally: but why not be content with this plurality of words appropriate to the diversity of the situations? Even allowing (at least for the sake of argument) that a justification for the word 'God' can be given by reference to distinctive situations reached by non-moral routes, why should the word 'God' predominate? Our answer could be two-fold: (i) A use of Occam's razor, which counsels us not to multiply beyond necessity, would suggest that we do something to keep ultimate concepts to a minimum. (ii) The traditional quest of metaphysics may be regarded as a search for unity at any rate in the sense that it aims at having some one ultimate concept by which to interpret the universe. The metaphysically minded at any rate will certainly look for some dominant category.

All to the good, then, if the word 'God' could integrate the various words and phrases which are attached to the diverse routes by which distinctive situations are evoked; and this in fact is what the believer in God – the holder of a metaphysical theology – sets out to do. He seeks to make 'God' the one

---

[1] See pp. 23-26 above, and also 'The Systematic Elusiveness of "I" ', *Philosophical Quarterly*, Vol. 5, No. 20, July 1955, pp. 193-204.

ultimate category, the key-word of his language. With these background considerations let us now close in on our particular problem. If we take 'God' as an ultimate category in this way, *how* do we in particular subordinate 'Duty' to 'God'. What connections do we build between the two concepts? Where do we find a language bridge? The answer is: in and from situations such as promise-making, where by an act of will I create an obligation. I promise to buy my boy a Dinky toy next month, and when it appears in the shop it becomes an obligation it would otherwise lack. Here I am, then, creating obligations by my promise-making; creating obligations by my decisions; creating obligations by my will. The suggestion then arises that we should link 'God' to an obligation word like 'Duty' by talking in terms of 'God's will'. But from the start we ought to remember that we use this picture of promises and my will only because we have nothing better to hand as a diagram by which to make our language bridge. And while it may give us a useful language link between 'Duty' and 'God', its more extensive use is fraught with danger. For as God is not 'I', neither can any and all stories about myself and my will, or other people and their wills, be transferred without great logical caution to God.

We cannot too strongly emphasise that while in speaking of 'God' and 'God's will' we have implied *some* logical kinship between 'God' and 'I', there cannot be identity of logical behaviour. God is not a man: he is as different from a man as 'infinitely wise' is from 'wise', and that difference I have tried to elucidate elsewhere.[1] The moral, for our present purpose, is that we must not develop *ad lib.* and without the greatest logical caution language about 'God's will'. Otherwise we are likely to raise all kinds of unnecessary difficulties, and to some of these we will now turn.

For instance, it has often been assumed that the following assertions were equivalents: (*a*) 'I ought to do X' (or 'It's my duty to do X'); (*b*) 'It is God's will that I should do X'; and

[1] *Religious Language*, pp. 65-71.

(*c*) 'God commands me to do X and will punish me if I do not.'
It has been argued, as Dr D. A. Rees has pointed out, that this
was the view, for example, of such philosophers as Locke and
Paley,[1] and we may readily agree that some believers in God,
not recognizing the peculiar logical status of the assertion (*b*)
have made what we shall argue is illegitimate, the transition
from (*b*) to (*c*); and in doing this they have been followed at least
by Ayer in the controversy we have mentioned earlier.

First then let us look at the alleged equivalence of (*a*) and (*b*).
Philosophers have often rejected it, but have they rejected such
an account of the relationship between (*a*) and (*b*) as we have
just given? For example, at one time C. D. Broad[2] and A. C.
Ewing[3] condemned it as 'theological naturalism', meaning very
roughly by this phrase that it confounded theology and ethics.
For, they argued in effect, the assertion (*a*) is of a logically
unique and autonomous kind, whereas the assertion (*b*) seems
some kind of straightforward, empirical assertion, albeit theological. We were therefore being offered as synonyms logically
diverse assertions, assertions in ethics and assertions in theology.
Such a criticism is in any case nowadays less disastrous than
once it seemed, if we are prepared to admit that, speaking
generally, assertions do not easily fall into very rigid and firmly
separable areas, and that in particular, in ethical assertions, the
factual and evaluative elements are very much intermingled.
But that answer aside – and this brings us back to our present
discussion – what we have suggested is something quite different. Our suggestion is that (*a*) and (*b*) are not to be taken as mere
synonymous substitutes (which might well open itself to the
criticism of Broad and Ewing). They are rather alternative and
complementary assertions viewing the same situation through
two different language frames.

What, however, of the alleged equivalence of (*b*) and (*c*)? It
is here, we would emphasise, that language about God's will is

[1] See D. A. Rees, 'The Ethics of Divine Commands', *Proceedings
of the Aristotelian Society*, New Series LVII, 1956-7, pp. 83-107.
[2] *Five Types of Ethical Theory*, London, 1930, p. 259.
[3] *The Definition of Good*, London, 1948, pp. 106-10, 111-14.

being expanded to a point where its illegitimate development becomes evident. For instance, if the child admits that 'It is my nurse's will that I should do X', he will naturally and rightly assert, 'My nurse commands me to do X and will punish me if I do not.' Again, if we say 'It is the sergeant-major's will that I should present arms', it will certainly follow that 'The sergeant-major commands me to present arms and will punish me if I do not.' But because 'It is God's will that I should do X' is grammatically like 'It is my nurse's will that I should do Y', or 'It is the sergeant-major's will that I should do Z', it *does not* follow that these logical assertions are logical kinsmen. They could only be so if there were no significant difference between God, my nurse and the sergeant-major. Some believers in God may have pictured God as a grim Nurse or a ruthless Sergeant-Major. But not all, or most. Most believers have recognised welcome differences. So it was with logical circumspection that we introduced the phrase 'God's will'. We cannot do justice to theological language unless we somehow preclude the deduction that God, like a nurse or sergeant-major, is a man with a 'will' who can therefore issue commands such as we know in the nursery or on the barrack square, and arranges for punishment, such as we know on our trousers or in the guardroom. It is in fact to preclude this sort of unqualified extension of language about 'will' that the believer in God, in his calmer and more reflective moments, insists in speaking of God's *inscrutable*, or *perfect*, *infinite* 'will'.[1]

Yet having said that, let us admit in all honesty that some sort of defence, not at all involving these logical blunders, might be given at any rate to talk about God's 'punishment'. For punishment can be regarded as a means of insisting on the moral inescapability of a certain obligation. Just as a promise confers, as we have seen, moral significance upon an otherwise morally neutral occasion, just as a promise makes the Dinky toy a focus of an obligation,[2] so retributive punishment may be regarded

[1] See my *Religious Language*, Ch. II, 'Models and Qualifiers'.
[2] See p. 39 above.

(whether rightly or wrongly does not concern us here) as a means whereby, when the moral claims of a certain occasion have been overlooked or rejected, a moral adjustment can be made by conferring moral significance on certain subsequent situations. A man in love with a woman overlooks or positively rejects the moral claims of her husband, and kills him to make life less troublesome, and an elopement to some South American republic even more necessary. But he is caught, and capital punishment is administered. The husband was killed in disregard of all moral claims; the suitor is killed in the name of Justice. Retributive punishment intends to transfer to a subsequent parallel situation the obligatory character that was set aside in an original situation. So when an eye is put out in a brawl, retribute punishment demands that the observable features of the situation shall be repeated, but this time with their moral challenge proclaimed: the second eye is put out *as a duty*. To talk of punishing B if he fails to do X or does Y, becomes then a means of calling attention to the inescapable moral claims of X, or some situation Z with which Y conflicts. For these moral claims of X or Z, if they are resisted or otherwise not acknowledged, are held to entail subsequently a duty to punish, in this way obtaining at the second move the moral recognition which was due to them, but denied them at the outset by the failure to do X or the success in doing Y. If someone avoids or resists the challenge of Duty, Duty (it is argued) must alternatively express itself in punishment. On this background, talk of God's punishment becomes a picturesque means of insisting that 'God's will' relates to moral obligations that one way or another are inescapable and will prevail. In this way it is possible to give important logical point to talk about punishment in relation to God: and if so it can stand. But the risk of being read off against the wrong kind of logical pattern, the risk of assimilating God to a sergeant-major, is enormous. The religious person needs to be particularly careful to match his language to his insights. That reflection allows us a further word in regard to the Russell-Ayer controversy.

What we said earlier rightly suggests that those who have claimed that only a religious standpoint would keep Lord Russell from his difficulties have in principle been correct. But unfortunately, they have often contrived to express their point in a way which, blind to its logical difficulties, asserted what was positively false. Without being alert to the delicate logical move implied in talking of Duty in terms of God's will, they have modelled God so closely on the nurse or sergeant-major pattern as to have no other reason for doing their duty than that to do otherwise would result in their being set across some celestial knee or brought before a cosmic court-martial. At the same time such mistakes do not in themselves invalidate the claim that belief in 'absolute values' is a religious belief, and if it is a religious belief it can *somehow* be talked of in terms of God. What we have tried to do has been to give some hints as to how such talking could be legitimately and more fruitfully developed. Our conclusion is that, avoiding assertions like 'God commands me to do X and will punish me if I do not' (which are more likely to be misread than to be found edifying), we may nevertheless say, in addition to saying that 'I ought to do X' and 'X is my duty', that 'X is God's will for me'. In saying this we are in fact using such a phrase as 'God's will' to give us an alternative description for what confronts us when we are aware of obligation, an alternative description which seeks to do justice to the fact that there are distinctive disclosure-situations other than those in which 'Duty' is pegged. So the one key word 'God' includes, and has a wider use than, the other key word 'Duty'. At this point we might well recall that it was only when he recognized pleasure as something logically distinct from Duty, yet equally to be interpreted with it, that Kant talked about God. It is from our point of view significant that Kant argued that the word 'God' was needed when, and only when, he had to bring together what for him were the two logically different languages of duty and pleasure. For us, likewise, the basic justification for having the word 'God' as well as the phrase 'Absolute Values' or 'Duty' is that the world contains more distinctive situations than those which characterise morality. 'Duty is God's will' is then analytic in the sense that whatever is 'God's will' will include, as a part, whatever is 'my Duty'. But whatever is 'God's will' includes much else besides: the existence, for example, of created beings, the procession of the seasons and so on. If we write, 'X is God's will', possible values for X will not only include terms from morality; they will include terms relating to all kinds of non-moral situations as well, e.g. we may say, '*The succession of seed-time and harvest* is God's will.'

There, then, is our answer – somewhat lengthy and complicated I fear – to the questions as to how belief in absolute values is related to belief in God, how talk about Duty is related to talk about God's will. Our suggestion is that part of the logical behaviour of the word 'God', and the phrase 'God's will', duplicates the logical behaviour of the word 'Duty' and the phrase 'absolute value'. Even so, we must emphasise (having in mind what Ayer said[1]) that this logical overlap is not properly expressed by talking of 'absolute ethical values' being 'validated by God'. Cruelty is not wrong because God forbids it. Good is not right because God commands it. To talk like this is to make the mistake of thinking of God as a Superior Sergeant-Major or a Great Nurse. The connection is rather one between alternative descriptions, one of which is contextually more comprehensive than the other. That remark can be given a final illustration which I hope will also show how bogus is the old dilemma: Is something my Duty because it is God's will, or is it God's will because it is my duty? Let us compare the two assertions: 'Duty is God's will' and $\frac{'x^2}{a^2} + \frac{y^2}{b^2} = 1$ is a conic section'. How pointless it would be to ask, 'Is it a conic section because it is $\frac{x^2}{a^2} + \frac{y^2}{b^2} = 1$, or is it $\frac{x^2}{a^2} + \frac{y^2}{b^2} = 1$ because it is a conic section?' It obviously depends on what context we opt for as a beginning. If we are

---

[1] See p. 44 above.

working with co-ordinate geometry, if we have started with axes and co-ordinates, we shall conclude that something is a conic section because it has this equation. On the other hand, if we begin with solid geometry, with conic sections made by a cutting plane, and try to find out how to talk about them in terms of axes and co-ordinates, we shall say that the equation is such and such because this is a conic section. The same is true about asking whether something is my duty because it is God's will, or whether it is God's will because it is my duty. The question is in fact a pseudo-question. But it has a point, and this point is to reveal that we have here two alternative descriptions, 'Duty' and 'God's will', between which some kind of logical priority waits to be established. So with the mathematics example. It will be found that the phrase 'conic section' covers many more *loci* than that of the ellipse whose equation we have given. 'Conic section' is a more extensive description. Likewise 'God's will'. The one phrase $\frac{x^2}{a^2} + \frac{y^2}{b^2} = 1$', or 'Duty' respectively might stand without the other – 'conic section', or 'God's will' respectively – but not *vice versa*. In this way, the former phrases are contextually less comprehensive than the latter.

So we may readily recognise that it is possible to talk of 'Duty' without speaking of 'God's will'; some do so talk and these include many humanists, and at best Lord Russell. Hence, even theists have rightly wanted to say that duties would exist even if *per impossibile* there were no God. This has been a picturesque way of describing in the material mode the one aspect of the logical relations between 'Duty' and 'God's will' which has just been formulated. But more needs saying, or so we would claim. On our view, it would not be possible to speak of 'God's will' without being logically committed to speaking of something as a 'Duty'. So it has happened that theists have also wished to say that the 'source' of all duty and absolute value is God. In saying this they have been wishing to assert from another direction the supremacy of the key phrase 'God's will' or of the word 'God', and again a logical relationship has taken on a picturesque expression in the material mode.

Here, then, is a treatment of Duty, absolute values and God's will, which I am bold to think avoids various difficulties which have arisen in the past. Some of these difficulties the Russell-Ayer controversy implied, others it made explicit.

3. *Freedom and Omnipotence*

We have already seen that along with a decision which is personal and free, there goes a challenge – a moral obligation – to which that decision is a response, and that while this challenge may be labelled 'Absolute Value' or 'Duty', it can also carry the more comprehensive description, 'God's will'. Now as freedom and obligation are in this way correlative concepts, so then are 'my freedom' and 'God's will'. Such a reflection can illuminate, I believe, the old problem of praise and omnipotence, to which I now come as my third and last corollary.

There is, let it first be noticed, an insoluble version of this problem which runs as follows. It begins with (say) a head-master who is a veritable terror. He makes all his staff work six out of the seven periods each day, and even on the seventh period he sends out secretarial spies to see that they are marking books in the Common Room or reading the *Science Masters' Journal*, or *Mathematical Pie*, or the latest circular about the Cadet Corps. On Sunday nights at 11.30 p.m. he will even ring up masters about this or that Staff meeting, or some difficult pupil. Here is the Headmaster all energetic and powerful, and it is plain that the Assistant Master has, consequentially, precious little freedom. But if this is true of some Headmaster, what now of (say) a Prime Minister? Who knows what oppression and lack of freedom the Cabinet Room at No. 10 has shown at periods when there have been powerful and dominating Prime Ministers? If the Prime Minister is all-powerful, the Cabinet Minister is completely overwhelmed and treated, indeed, as a child. But even the most powerful Prime Minister is not God. How then can we be free?

Here, then, is the insoluble version of the problem, suggesting that all-powerfulness and freedom are incompatible.

But can we be sure that this picture, into which the problem has been translated, is the correct one? When we speak of God as all-powerful in this way, are we using a reliable logical map for reading off our theological geography? Is this what is meant by speaking of God as 'all-powerful'?

'God is all-powerful.' Let it be said at once that if we are to do logical justice to this assertion, we must obviously make sure that it is anchored in a religious situation, which means that we must somehow relate it to the kind of situation we have been talking about in the case of duty. If, for instance, we began by assimilating 'all-powerful' to 'very powerful' or 'exceedingly powerful', as though grammatical similarity of itself brought logical kinship, we would have taken from the phrase at the start the religious significance we should then, in vain, attempt to give it. If we began by equating God and the Prime Minister, there would be no limit to the problems we might generate and discuss, but the discussion would be theologically quite irrelevant. So denying such assimilation, let us look for a different account altogether of the logical structure of the phrase 'all-powerful'. Let us not assimilate it to 'excessively powerful'. My suggestion is that we regard 'all-powerful' as what I have called elsewhere[1] a qualified model. What now is a 'qualified model'? Our answer begins by claiming that, of the two words 'all' and 'powerful', one of them – in this case 'powerful' – sets before us a model, something with which we are perfectly familiar. Here is a word about whose meaning everyone, believer and unbeliever, philosopher and man-in-the-street, can agree. So we call 'powerful' a model because it specifies a familiar situation by means of which there can be given to us eventually an understanding of what is at the moment puzzling or problematical, i.e. the phrase 'all-powerful' as used in religious language. For instance, when we say the word 'power' perhaps there

[1] *Religious Language*, esp. Ch. II, and see also pp. 92-99 of the present book.

57

comes to mind civil power, of which, in principle, a complete account could be given in purely 'object' terms. Civil power is something easily translatable into fines, prisons, executions and the sword. It is described appropriately as the 'arm of the law', for it talks of no more than the spatio-temporal. But then we see the limitations of such power. We remember the familiar proverb: 'The pen is mightier than the sword.' So for a model of greater power we are led to contemplate (say) the power of literary composition, the power the novelist can exert on his readers. For example, Dickens. But the point might now be made that Dickens would have been even more powerful if he had lived an attractive moral life as well. The novelist's power is then even greater if to it is added the power of moral example as well. But what is that still greater power which influences the exemplar? We now begin to speak of the power exercised by duty. And what can prove even more powerful than duty? The answer might be that, going beyond duty, is the power of love. Then, what sort of love? Never-failing. And so on. . . . For no story which terminates can talk of a love which never does.

Now it is my contention that the logical function of the word 'all' is to act as a qualifier, as an operator, which directs us in this sort of way to survey examples of greater and greater power which can be continued as far as we like . . . until there breaks in on us at some point, no matter where, a challenge which goes beyond the objects. We have then a characteristically religious situation of whose objective aspect, as in the case of duty, we may use the word 'God'. Here is the situation explicating and justifying the assertion that God is all-powerful. Incidentally, such a situation as a whole is commonly called one of worship, and what we have just done is in fact to outline the logical structure of Whitehead's famous dictum that the power of God is the worship he inspires.[1]

Now, as we have just noticed, the challenge of such a situation is the same kind of challenge that I acknowledge when I

[1] *Science and the Modern World*, Cambridge, 1933 ed., Ch. XII, p. 239.

recognise my Duty. We speak indeed of love exerting a compelling power, and of the dutiful behaviour which should issue from worship. To practise θρησκεία καθαρά – wholesome worship, rites and ceremonies – is, says St James, to visit the fatherless and widows in their affliction.[1] . . . The conclusion is that to the 'all-powerfulness' of God, as to the obligations of Duty, we respond 'freely'. Our response has our personal backing. In both cases – whether in discerning the all-powerfulness of God, or in discerning our Duty – we are never more 'ourselves' than we are then. We are 'free' precisely when we can say that God is 'omnipotent'. Indeed, we shall only know what we mean by the one phrase when we also know what we mean by the other. Man's freedom and God's omnipotence are no more incompatible than freedom and obligation: indeed, in both cases, we have correlative phrases. The kind of situation which justifies man's freedom, justifies at the same time God's omnipotence. The problem of 'man's freedom' and 'God's omnipotence' is thus a pseudo-problem which disappears when the appropriate logical placings are given to each phrase.

But, the reader may say, this is to solve the problem of 'freedom' and 'omnipotence' by giving the words new meanings; just as by a similar device 'democracy' and 'Communism' can be made to look compatible. The cases, however, are not at all parallel. In the latter case (or so it is argued) 'democracy' has a perfectly clear and accepted meaning which, far from having difficulties of its own, fits compactly into a certain world-view. The word is then taken from this acknowledged location and used in an incompatible world-view, given a radically different contextual setting, and thus given a radically different meaning.

The theological case is quite different. It is true that to reconcile freedom and omnipotence has been for long a theological problem, just as for some, the reconciliation of 'democracy' and 'Communism' is a hardy annual. But there the similarity stops. No one has ever been very clear as to what 'freedom' or 'omnipotence' have meant. There is no question

[1] James 1.27.

of anyone having firm and accepted meanings for these words, or if they have had, it has been, as I have tried to show, within a very restricted context, viz. on a model which did no justice to what religious people have meant by God. There is no question of 'freedom' and 'omnipotence' having wholly acceptable placings in some world view. Each has been set in the most fragmentary contexts. What we have tried to do is not to give the words new meanings, but to indicate a wider context in which both words can be used without denying their previous insights, but where the problem of their relationship disappears. It is not so much a new (still less, as in the case of democracy and Communism, an obviously incompatible) meaning, that we have given the concepts, but a further elucidation which permits of logical links that the earlier fragmentary contexts denied, or at least left problematical. What we have tried to do has been to give to 'freedom' and 'omnipotence' not new meaning, but wider location which allows the words to be used very largely as they have always been, but which also enables us to banish the problem of freedom and omnipotence. Our claim is that once freedom and omnipotence are seen as the religious words they are, to be grounded in a distinctive situation, the problem of their relationship, which arose on a mistaken allocation, is solved, solved as problems always are solved (if they are soluble) by referring concepts back to their empirical grounds, by going back to the 'facts' themselves.

How careful, then, we must be not to sponsor inadequate or mistaken logical allocations. What disastrous reasoning can follow from thinking of responsible decision wholly in terms of causal determinism, from thinking of God wholly in terms of a sergeant-major or a battle-axe headmaster. It may be that some theological doctrines – some of those to do with predestination and the like – have pictured God as though the Prime Minister or Potentate model were wholly appropriate. But apart from other difficulties, not the least logical blunder which such doctrines make is that they confound 'persons' and people,[1] and

[1] As do certain arguments against immortality, see pp. 65ff below.

peg religious language to situations which do not extend beyond the objects they contain.

Let us now survey the course of our argument in this chapter. I began with three examples, the road accident, the Good Samaritan and the booking clerk, which were all designed to show that a free decision is not just a reaction to stimuli but involves all that and something more besides, something which makes it all the more appropriate to speak of it as a response to a challenge, a challenge which is the challenge of 'objects' and more. I then continued these examples with others illustrating a distinction between what I called a 'plain' and a 'responsible' decision, and these illustrations were meant to develop further the point that this challenge, to which a responsible decision is a response, is a challenge which, like the decision itself, cannot be constrained in object language. It is a challenge which holds 'for better for worse; for richer for poorer . . .', a challenge which is never netted in any one empirical circumstance or its opposite, for it includes and goes beyond them all. In this way a transcendent decision is a response to a transcendent object. Freedom is correlative with obligation.

We then discussed three corollaries:

1. We saw how futile it must be to talk of this transcendent response in causal language. For causal terms are only appropriate for relations between objects, and this response is distinctive precisely in so far as it needs more than the language of 'objects' to talk about it.

2. I then showed how, against this background, we might resolve the kind of conflict which arises between the humanist who believes in Absolute Values, and the theist who believes in God as the 'source' of such values. Continuing the discussion, I next suggested how we could rightly understand such an assertion as 'Duty is God's will', so as to avoid problems which arise from giving to such an assertion a mistaken logical structure, problems that arise when we misread its grammar.

3. Finally, I showed how there is no more a problem of reconciling man's freedom and God's omnipotence than there

is a problem of reconciling man's freedom and his sense of obligation. Both are correlates. Once again, we have an example of the futilities and bogus difficulties which can arise if we persist in mistaken logical allocations.

III

IMMORTALITY: PERSONS

W E STARTED our discussion of freedom by concentra-
ting on the character of decision. Even though there
can be what we might call 'impersonal' decision –
doing this rather than that, actualising one possibility instead
of another, behaving like the bagatelle ball – there can also be
given to such a decision a personal backing, and such 'personal'
decisions are then 'free' as not being restricted to, or exhaustively described in terms of, the 'objects' which characterise
them. We then do not behave like a battle-axe; we act as a
'person'. Further, such decision occurs as a response to a
challenge, the challenge of duty or obligation, which likewise
cannot be constrained by the language of 'objects'. In such cases
we have a 'responsible' decision. Here is the doctor who responds to the call of duty, the booking clerk who recognises and
chases the criminal. Here is the case of marriage, where whatever its social, psychological and biological conditioning, there
is a mutual decision to accept each other 'for better, for
worse . . .', the promise of a loyalty whatever the empirical
circumstances.

So the situation claimed by the doctrine of free will concerns
subjectively that kind of decision in which a person transcends
his public behaviour and acts more than 'officially', and this as
response to a challenge which *objectively* equally transcends
public terms. We saw how, on this background, we might clarify
and settle the points at issue between the humanist and the
theist, and become clearer about the relation of duty to God's

will. Finally, the fact that freedom and obligation are set together within one situation enables us to avoid the pseudo-problem which is generally expressed in terms of a conflict between human freedom and God's omnipotence. Here, then, is a justifiable way of using language about freedom and God.

I hope now to show that it is in a similar way that the language about immortality can be defended, that the language of immortality can be justified by reference to the situations similar to those we have been considering already. The suggestion is already growing more plausible that it is by reference to such situations that many of the traditional concepts of metaphysics and philosophical theology will be given their meaning and defence, when we take up the challenge of contemporary empiricism.[1]

What, then, is this situation in relation to which immortality is to be understood and belief in immortality thereby defended? Let us approach it through a difficulty which is a somewhat modern difficulty. 'Death' (it is said) means 'the end of life'; therefore the phrase 'life after death' is meaningless. It is as though we said that since 'Penzance' is the name given to the most south-westerly end of the Western Region of British Railways, then it inevitably follows that such a phrase as 'south-westerly travel on the Western Region beyond "Penzance" ' is meaningless, talking of nothing whatever.

To see what lies behind the difficulty let us develop it somewhat, and begin by recognising that the word 'death' can have many meanings. Biological 'death', for example, will inevitably involve talk of certain biochemical reactions, a breakdown of organic processes, decomposition, and all such stories as are a commonplace in the lecture rooms and laboratories of physiology, pathology and the rest. Again, 'death', for the psychologist, is that point beyond which we never again show the appropriate behaviour responses. Socially, 'death' is that occasion after which a man no longer throws his darts or his dinner parties. 'Death' for the statistician is something which involves the

[1] See Introduction, p. 12.

pay-out of insurance premiums. 'Death' for the undertaker is what keeps him busy, enabling him to be cheerful, if not too cheerful. In all these cases 'death' does in fact tell of the 'end of life'. So it has been said[1] that, taking people as what we meet, touch and see, who walk and talk with us, serve us with meat and, if we are lucky with our butcher, joke with us as well, we cannot talk significantly about these 'people' – those who do all this talking and joking – living after death. For death ends everything which is now taken to characterise their behaviour.

Now as we have repeatedly urged in the first two chapters, it is true that people *can* and do occur in 'impersonal' situations, situations which can be exhaustively described in terms of 'objects', situations which consist wholly of public behaviour. People *are* impersonal in so far as they can be classified on identity cards as NWPC/163/2, or card-indexed in the Services G/JX/3568234, or given descriptive names such as 'the butcher', the 'tax collector', the 'battle-axe doctor', the 'booking clerk', and even (as we saw) the priest and the Levite. The crucial question is: Are we ever more than all this? The argument that 'life after death' is a meaningless phrase, is unanswerable if each one of us can be exhaustively described in terms of his public behaviour. Here then is the crucial question. Are we merely our biochemical reactions, our organic processes, our behaviour responses, our social graces and disgraces, our economic significance to the insurance broker, work for the undertaker, *or more*?

Now at this point we might have a discussion on nicknames – those words which have a minimum spatio-temporal reference, but which can nevertheless become the currency for the most intimate personal transactions. There are occasions, it is true, when a nickname such as 'Redhead' may be no more than the picking out of some prominent feature of some person or other

---

[1] Especially by Professor A. G. N. Flew. See e.g. *New Essays in Philosophical Theology*, London, 1955. Ch. XV. The reader may also wish to see his article, 'Can a man witness his own funeral?', *Hibbert Journal*, LIV, April 1956, pp. 242-50, and an article by the present author, 'Persons and Funerals: what do person words mean?', in the same journal (July 1956, pp. 330-8).

and the use of this as a convenient shorthand to denote him. The nickname, in such circumstances, would not for our present purpose be at all significant. But there are nicknames and nicknames, and we might more profitably have in mind what is perhaps not so much a nickname as a pet name, where again some characteristic or feature, by itself trivial, is fixed upon and used as a symbol for what the person means to us more than the impersonal behaviour he displays. At home, even the tax-collector may be 'Buster', and to his family the Divisional Gas Manager may be only 'Old Smell'.

Or again, we might recall that all our discussions of freedom were an endeavour to show that no matter how much of our behaviour is impersonal, there are nevertheless decision-situations, such as when we respond to obligations, when we display a moral response which is not a causal reaction, where our behaviour is not restricted to the spatio-temporal patterns which characterise it. So we could say that the person who is 'free' is, at the moment of his 'free decision', 'alive', never more 'himself' than he is then. Further, *this* sense of 'life' is *not* one which death, as a descriptive word, ends. For 'life' now refers to a situation which is not exhausted by any one or all of a set of spatio-temporal events. In the same sort of way, anyone who says, 'I had only half decided at noon yesterday', is saying in this sense of 'alive', 'I was only half alive at noon yesterday'. As for the person who makes no moral decisions at all, then he is no person at all, he is no 'man', he is inhuman. 'Life after death' for such a being is certainly meaningless. We may recall what the existentialists so often tell us, that the retired 'official' – if he has been nothing more than an 'official' – is dead already.

So to justify 'freedom' by appealing to decision-situations which exceed public behaviour, and even to recall one use of nicknames, is, at the same time to justify belief in immortality. For to do either shows that we are not restricted or confined to those features of our existence which are in space and time. Because we are in that sense 'free', in that sense we are 'immortal'.

It is not of course my intention merely to repeat the claims

66

of earlier chapters, and to make four chapters from the substance of two. So questions of freedom and nicknames apart, what I want to do in this chapter is:

1. First, to show that typical arguments *against* immortality[1] derive their point from stressing our public, 'impersonal' behaviour, and from restricting and belittling our 'personal' significance. Their aim is so to emphasize and insist on the public character of our behaviour, as to avoid evoking the kind of situation we have been concerned to stress and which we would argue is the empirical basis for immortality.

2. Secondly and contrariwise, I hope to show that arguments *for* immortality[1] can be viewed as techniques to evoke a more-than-objects, more-than-public-behaviour, kind of situation. Further, having our discussion of freedom in mind, we shall not be surprised if one of these arguments – that from considerations of duty – echoes something of our earlier discussions.

First, then, let us see how many typical arguments *against* immortality can be viewed as inhibitive or repressive in their function.. It is sometimes argued that the circumstances of human birth and death are totally inappropriate to an immortal being. What of a child, it is said, born from a drunken revelry, or blown to pieces by accidentally touching a hidden and unexploded bomb which someone's carelessness has left about? Or again (the argument continues) is not human life continuous with that of dogs, worms, fleas and amoeba, and is it not possible to tell very convincing biological stories linking all these inextricably together? Have we then to suppose that worms, fleas and amoeba are immortal? Yet if *they* are not immortal and life is continuous between them and us, how can we suppose that *we* are immortal? Or again (it is said) would not immortality make the universe too crowded? Is there room for everyone to survive? If everyone everywhere, at all times, survived, would not the second-class compartment of a business train to London

[1] For an excellent and clear survey of such arguments, the reader is referred to *The Mind and its Place in Nature*, London, 1925, Chs. XI, XII. In these chapters details of all the arguments I use will be found, with Dr C. D. Broad's independent discussion of their merits.

Bridge, or of an excursion train from Oldham to Blackpool, be, by comparison with the future life, as empty as the desert?

From an opposite direction, counter-arguments are now developed. Against the first objection, it is emphasized that birth and death arise from a very complex pattern of cause factors, and we cannot be justified in judging their significance from one or a few of these cause factors which happen at the time to be the most obvious and striking. As to the argument from continuity, continuity can well be allowed between the first and last terms of a series without having to suppose that the endpoints – the first and last terms – have identical characteristics. The continuity which there undoubtedly is between the Brylcreem youth and the baldheaded septuagenarian, does not compel us to say that each has the same head of hair. As to the difficulty of finding room for everybody in a future life, we need only remind ourselves, the counter-argument continues, of the vastness of the universe. Where are its limits?

Now it is not my purpose to develop such arguments and counter-arguments with the intention of leaving the matter wholly in the air and the reader at best sceptical of both positions. Nor are we interested in the details of these arguments and counter-arguments as such. It is far more important from our point of view to see what the arguments are in fact claiming and counterclaiming. It is far more important to see the differing claims to which each set of arguments is attached.

The arguments against immortality are plainly intent on emphasizing the impersonal and the no-more-than-natural features of human existence. They try to deny or belittle our personal significance, and to debunk what at first sight is a situation of mystery and wonder. Birth (for example) is set before us as a sort of daily round in the world regarded as a casual and rather ill-arranged breeding station, with men and women – drink-filled or not – performing the same exercises in sexual reproduction as characterise farmyard animals. How is there anything immortal here? The child's body is blown to pieces without trace: how can there be any trace of his personality? Nature is so often callous and casual: are not her products the same? How like fleas – some of us performing fleas – we all are! And if we picture immortality at all, we are to picture it apparently with humanity crushed and huddled together like sardines in a tin. What could be less visionary? The whole intention of these arguments against immortality is to atrophy all vision or wonder, and to make our existence, here or any-where else, drab and superficial, to make us 'objects' and no more.

On the other side, the technique of counter-arguments has a contrary purpose. It endeavours, contrariwise, to evoke wonder and to deepen our vision. The counter-arguments will be wise to deny no facts which the other arguments have set out. But each time they will claim that what the other argument puts forward is *not* the whole story. Animal and human reproduction may in many ways be very similar. Some births and deaths may seem nothing but events in an inexorable causal process. Nature may seem callous and casual. But (the argument now continues) birth and death tell of something much more complex than physiology reckons with – there is this and that feature . . . and that . . . and that . . . and the argument will continue this story till the penny drops, and the light dawns, and we see what 'more' there is in any birth and death than the scientific factors and causal patterns which undoubtedly characterise each.

Again, we may well recognise our biological kinship with dogs, worms, fleas, and amoeba, but what the counter-argument now does, by emphasising the differences which characterise even the members of continuous series, is to try to call attention to the point at which we are dogs *and more*, worms *and more*, fleas *and more*, amoeba *and more*, and not just 'more' in being bigger and more complex organisms, though we are indeed that. As for the overcrowded universe, again we tell a story without ending – this time the story of how the universe goes on, and on, and on. . . . Again the hope is that there will be evoked at some point or other in this unending story, that in which our immortality is founded, a situation which while being spatio-temporal is more than spatio-temporal.

Let me emphasise again that my point has *not* been to give a detailed assessment of the arguments against immortality, still less of the counter-arguments. Much more would need to be said if that were so. My purpose has been rather to display the crucial point which is at issue between the arguments, and which I believe comes to this: that whether or not we believe in immortality depends on whether or not we recognise a certain kind of situation, which the arguments we first outlined tried to deny, and which the counter-arguments in their turn tried to evoke.

Let us now look at some typical arguments *for* immortality, with the same purpose in mind; we will divide them into three classes:

    (i) arguments from duty;
    (ii) arguments based on the results of psychical research;
    (iii) other empirical arguments.

(i) Certain duties imply (it is said) immortality. For example (the argument goes) there is no point in devoting our lives to the search for truth, or exhausting our energies in a moral struggle for perfection, if we are to be completely snuffed out at three score years and ten, when we shall certainly not have reached our target. Surely it would be much wiser in such circumstances to concentrate on 'immediate pleasure', knowing, if not the world, at least the shadier part of it. So the fact that we recognise a duty to search for truth, and a duty to press on morally towards perfection, demands that we are immortal. If we were not immortal there would be no point in doing either. The argument thus claims that there are certain 'unattainable' duties to seek perfection of one sort or another which, so to say, make sense, which we recognise as obligations, and which at the same time we have no chance here and now to fulfil. Therefore, if we are to take such duties seriously, we must be immortal.

At this point two difficulties are often raised.

(*a*) Do these duties necessarily demand immortality? We

might still wish, it is argued, to pursue knowledge even if we knew we were mortal, and even if we recognised that we should never attain perfect knowledge. We might even defend our pursuit by pointing to its useful social implications for our contemporaries and successors, or we might be content merely to emphasise the joys of the chase itself. Even if we were all mortal, it does not follow that we would wish to make asses of ourselves. Even if 'tomorrow we die', it does *not* follow that we shall wish to spend today eating and drinking. A scientist in Oxford might still wish to spend his last day in the labs. rather than in 'The King's Arms'.

(*b*) The other difficulty is this. Do we (it is asked) know any of these duties to be duties at all without having to know first that we are immortal? If so, even if the argument were formally valid, it would be quite worthless. For the argument would then fail in what W. E. Johnson called its 'epistemic' conditions: we should have to know the conclusion before we could entertain the premiss, whereas for a satisfactory inference, the original premiss, the ground of the inference, must be *independently* known. An example will illustrate this logical point. The inference:

   (i) The King is supreme.
  (ii) The Prime Minister depends on his majority in parliament.
∴ (iii) The King is not the Prime Minister.

is valid and useful because we can know (i) without having first to know (iii). On the other hand, the inference:

   (i) Nature is uniform.
  (ii) Potassium nitrate when heated yesterday gave off oxygen.
∴ (iii) Potassium nitrate on heating will always give off oxygen.

is formally valid, but quite useless because we could not know (i) without first knowing (iii).

71

Is it the case, then, that recognition of these 'unattainable' duties only follows belief in immortality, or at least is only given along with it? If so, the argument under consideration would be valueless, for we could not know the ground of the inference, viz. that so and so is a duty, before we knew the conclusion of the inference, viz. that we are immortal.

But at this point I think the light begins to break. For the second difficulty emphasises that what is being claimed by the positive argument is that, in some way or another, and at any rate in some cases, our awareness of obligation and our awareness of immortality are given together. Now this reflection enables us, I think, to see the true character of the argument. What it is trying to do is to use an ethical technique, viz. to tell a duty story, in the hope of evoking the kind of situation in which our conviction of immortality is grounded. Let us illustrate this technique in rather more detail before going back to consider the two difficulties we have just formulated. We might picture it as a three-stage technique:

(1) First we call up a behaviour pattern labelled 'seeking immediate pleasure', 'eating and drinking', where drinking is talked of in terms of throat membranes, stomach capacity and digestive juices. The picture is – quite crudely – of a throat being tickled by half a pint of lemonade or Double Diamond. There is no immortality here: everything is as impersonal as the tongues and the intestines in the jars in the anatomy laboratory.

(2) On this impersonal picture we then superimpose a duty story, and for the moment the mention of any kind of duty will do. The throat is being tickled in the inn when someone runs in: – 'A child is drowning outside!' . . . and the whole scene comes to life, takes on 'depth'. Parallel with the example in Chapter II, we must not now suppose that this is merely a case of efficient reaction to stimuli, but that the people speak of 'being compelled' to rush out and with an 'inward' compulsion, etc. etc. They would speak of being 'obliged' to dive in for the child.[1]   [1] See p. 30 above.

Now the contrast between such a situation and that which occurs at stage (1) may be enough to evoke a situation where we discern and recognise duty. That, in fact, was our hope when we used this sort of story in Chapter II. And it is in so recognising duty as something which transcends the spatio-temporal, that we recognise our own transcendence of the spatio-temporal, our own immortality. On the other hand, the light may not dawn, nor the penny drop.

(3) In such a case a story of so-called unattainable duties comes to its own. For whenever such a duty story as we have outlined at stage (2) does not work, these other stories of unattainable duties enable the technique to be continued and practised for as long as we wish. In the case of unattainable duties, the story can always be pressed further. It can always continue until the light dawns, and it would continue like this.

We could begin, for example, with a scholar who after many years of writing and research, returns to tell us, 'At last! I have completed my twentieth volume on the Nagi tribes of India.' Has he found the Truth? Has he exhausted an unattainable duty? 'No', we say. 'What you have done is a magnificent contribution to the search for truth, but the search has scarcely yet begun. Disheartening as it may seem, you have hardly begun to pick up, Newton-like, a pebble on the sea-shore.' Our scholar returns years later with yet more volumes. But the answer is the same. No matter when or with what results our imaginary scholar returned, we could still say, 'But you have not yet reached the whole truth, *the* Truth.' And then the light may dawn: then it may become plain what '*the* Truth' stands for – something which no volumes, however many, can complete, something to which no true story, however long, can do justice. It stands for something which no scholar, however skilled or hardworking, could formulate and describe. In this sense it is unattainable – unattainable in terms of discursive knowledge. Yet in another sense we have recognised it already. For we know what 'the Truth' means when the light dawns. It is only its formulation which is a never-ending task. We are reminded of the old Idealist phrase that what is ever 'Real' is nevertheless always 'waiting to be realised'. But the very fact that in this way 'the Truth' eludes any discursive enumeration, however long, shows its character, that it is something we understand by reference to a situation which is 'objects' and more. In this way never-ending stories about searching after truth become an appropriate technique for evoking a situation which, when it breaks in on us, we shall then call '*the* Truth', and see its challenge as one of Duty. And when that happens, we likewise know ourselves as transcending the spatio-temporal, never exhaustively described by object stories. We are assured of our immortality.

So it is that a description of the never-ending search for knowledge will be a useful technique to evoke a situation which transcends the spatio-temporal while it includes it, a situation which subjectively assures me of my immortality.[1]

So what might be evoked at stage (2), and what stage (3) need never despair of reaching, is a situation never exhaustively treated by 'true' propositions about observables, no matter how complex and developed that treatment may be. Here is a situation which subjectively and objectively transcends the spatio-temporal. Subjectively, here is the ground of our immortality, and objectively we have once again what is meant by Duty.

Let us round off our account of this three-stage technique with another example. Jimmy, an enthusiastic schoolboy, learns his tables, his chemical reactions, his dates, his conjugations and declensions, with avidity. He wishes to know 'what's true' in mathematics, science, history. He wishes to say 'what's true' in all his languages. One table leads to another, and the tables to formulae which grow ever more complex. Starting with one or two elements, the quest goes ever forward – from one element to another, from one radical to another, from inorganic to organic, etc. etc. One period of British history leads to another: but there is always European history to follow, American history and institutions thereafter . . . and as to languages – modern,

---

[1] Cp. our discussion on the language for immortality, p. 114ff.

medieval, oriental, and after languages, dialects. . . . The search
for truth becomes ever wider. But Jimmy the prodigy learns on.
Yet he learns all (as we might say) parrot-fashion. More and
more he builds up his knowledge – a veritable walking encyclopaedia. He wins television competitions so often that they have
to pay him to refrain from competing. But is this the end? Has
he now attained perfect knowledge? No – a new dialect has been
discovered in furthest Tibet, something new has been discovered
about crystal dislocation. And then one day, the light dawns –
he comes to himself, as we would say, and all he has learnt falls
into a pattern that symbolises something with which he feels
kinship. Here is what he has been searching for, the Truth
which is all possible truths and more, whose translation into
truths he can still continue to pursue. But henceforward Jimmy
is a parrot *and more*, a walking encyclopaedia *and more*. He has
(we repeat) come to himself. He has discerned his immortality,
his transcendence of the spatio-temporal. In discerning the
Truth, he has discerned this in himself as well.

Against the standpoint of this discussion let us now see the
significance of the two objections to this argument for immortality which we mentioned above.

(*a*) The question was: Do any duties demand immortality?
Surely we might wish (it was said) to pursue knowledge even
if we knew we were mortal. Now when it is said that we might
still want to pursue truth, whether we are immortal or not, that
we might still wish to devote our last day to some organic
synthesis or to the office files rather than having a continuous
feast, the point must of course be admitted and agreed. But at
the same time it has to be recognised that this *wish* need not
arise from a response to anything like Duty. What we did in the
lab. or in the office merely to gratify a wish, would not at all be
an activity including but transcending the objects it contained.
Two people might still elect to do the same organic experiment
as a way of passing the last day. But for one it might be no more
than gratification of a wish: a matter of mixing the reagents,
distillation and the rest, when there would be no response to

Duty and no intimation of immortality. For another, however, it could be not only the gratification of a wish, but also a response to Duty, a response to the Truth, a response to a discernment. There would then be a vision made up of reagents *and more*, distillation *and more*; and subjectively there would be a recognition of one's self as more than an organic chemist. The organic synthesis would now do more than exemplify a wish, it would symbolise and portray Duty, as well, and the chemist would have an intimation of immortality.

The contrast is then between, on the one hand, merely eating and drinking, merely spending days in the lab., merely poring over problems, merely writing treatises; and on the other hand doing precisely any or all of these, but within a situation which subjectively and objectively transcends objects while it contains them. To express the contrast as the argument often does, as one between duty and pleasure, is misleading. The contrast is rather between pleasure, and pleasure *plus*.

(*b*) We can see, too, how the problem of priorities arises. If our account is correct, our sense of duty and our sense of immortality belong together: to discern our duty is to discern our immortality, and *vice versa*. To recognise our immortality (subjectively) is also to recognise (objectively) a Duty never exhausted in object language, and therefore spoken of as 'unattainable', being never adequately portrayed as a pattern in space and time. Again, if once we recognise a Duty, e.g. the pursuit of truth or the search for perfection, whose spatio-temporal translation is never ending, which happens when a Duty situation has been evoked by stories of an 'unattainable' duty, the same situation reveals our immortality. In this way, there is no absolute *logical* priority between immortality and unattainable duty, and there is an intimate psychological connection. So we can readily see how it comes to be alleged that we only recognise such and such as a duty when we recognise ourselves as immortal. We can easily see how the argument comes to fail over the epistemic condition. But this does not mean that the argument for immortality from the existence of certain duties is valueless.

Indeed, it may be said that in the very fact that the epistemic conditions cannot be fulfilled lies the possibility of the 'argument' being valuable at all. For all the 'argument' hopes to do is so to talk about certain duties that there arises a discernment of immortality which for those 'with eyes to see' cannot have been there from the start. Even so, talk about epistemic conditions is not without its point. For it properly reminds us that we are not looking on the argument for immortality from duty as taking us on a deductive journey which will at the end lead us to assent to the logical subsequent proposition that we are immortal. We are not led to a proposition which pictures the facts, describing a quality called 'immortality' which belongs to some 'thing' called a 'soul',[1] as longevity may characterise a tortoise. Contrariwise, we take a much looser view of the function of argument and a much different view as to the anchorage of metaphysical words such as 'soul' and 'immortality'. Argument and counter-argument in discussions about immortality are rather stories whose intention is either to evoke or to deny a certain kind of situation. If someone did not recognise as a duty the search for truth and perfection, but knew first that he was immortal, the argument would certainly be useless and unnecessary as an 'argument' for immortality. Yet it might now be useful in the opposite direction: to show us that with belief in immortality went necessarily a recognition of duty as something which could 'never' (i.e. in terms of spatio-temporal behaviour) be fulfilled. If, however, it be countered that (as a third case) there might be someone who could contemplate and assent to the proposition that if he were immortal it would follow that he had such and such duties, or to the proposition that if he recognised such and such duties it would follow that he were immortal, without believing either that he was immortal or that he has such duties – when the argument would be quite useless all round – I should doubt it. For I should argue that a recognition of certain duties and a discernment of immortality are only seen to imply one another when each

[1] See further, pp. 100ff.

relates to a common situation which subjectively and objectively transcends the spatio-temporal. In short, and without prejudice to any general theory of implication, I am saying that we should not see *this* implication between duty and immortality without recognising certain behaviour as our duty on the one hand, and our immortality on the other. Indeed, the 'argument' is but talk to get us to see this implication and the situation in which it is founded.

The next argument, with which we can deal much more briefly, points to the wasted effort, the unrewarded goodness and the frustrations with which human lives abound. We may think of the man who quite devotedly year by year cuts and trims his garden hedge and with the same loving care tends his garden, yet on his death the next occupier neglects hedge and garden alike. Or there are mothers who spend their lives training children who grow up to be utterly thankless. Again, we may think of the kindness and thoughtfulness and generosity which is rejected, spurned, or evil spoken of. What sustains people through all this (the argument runs) is the conviction that some day – though beyond this present life – justice will prevail, that the universe is, on a long-term view, good and fair.

But the objection is then made that while the argument might prove immortality *if* there were also prior belief in God, yet without such a belief or some comparable belief, the argument proves nothing.

How are we to assess such criticisms? First let us reiterate that what the positive argument sets out to do is to evoke a situation which exceeds all the public behaviour it contains. This it does by a technique which concentrates on human struggles and frustrations, the partial character of our lives, our own finitude. All the stories used by the argument are attempts to evoke a situation which is transitory and more, spatio-temporal and more, by pointing to the 'unsatisfactoriness' of what is transitory. All the stories are attempts to evoke a sense of the permanent, a sense of what abides, by arousing in us a profound discontent with the changes and chances of a fleeting world.

On this interpretation it is not surprising – and this we would say is the important point behind the criticism just mentioned above – that belief in God has in fact always been closely associated with belief in immortality. For it is the same kind of situation which justifies both beliefs[1]; which reflection leads to a further suggestion. On our view it would be natural to suppose that if either belief was very dominant the other belief might be overlooked and even disappear altogether. This in fact is what has happened. People have often been quite satisfied with what has been given to them either objectively or subjectively in a disclosure situation, and have cared nothing for further complications. The Old Testament, for example, is significant in having from the first a belief in God and only much later (and let us notice it was when personal and responsible decision was more and more emphasised) stirrings of immortality. Before that time the Hebrews thought primarily of God, and of their 'solidarity', of their group-life. They were too outward-looking, too little concerned with themselves as 'persons' to be concerned about their immortality. The philosopher McTaggart, on the other hand, is an interesting example of a somewhat opposite emphasis. Though he accepted the immortality of persons, he would not agree that such an immortality situation as is specified by his use of the word 'love' needed any further reference to the God of traditional belief. Indeed he rather suggested that traditional belief in God compromised and impoverished belief in immortality.[2] McTaggart and the Hebrews were thus alike in seeing one half – though in each case a different half – of the whole truth. For it is one and the same situation which subjectively justifies belief in immortality and objectively justifies belief in God. Belief in God and belief in immortality fit together and find their anchorage in the same kind of situation.

Returning now to our main theme, the suggestion is that the

[1] See *Religious Language*, Ch. II, pp. 50-53.
[2] See e.g. *Some Dogmas of Religion*, London, 1906, Ch. VIII; *The Nature of Existence*, Cambridge, 1921, Vol. II, Ch. XLII; *Studies in Hegelian Cosmology*, Cambridge, 1901, Chs. ii, iii and ix, esp. iii § 94 and ix § 308.

old-fashioned ethical arguments for immortality are best understood (1) as techniques to evoke a particular and distinctive kind
of situation, which (2) at the same time claims from the way in
which the situation is evoked, that such a situation exceeds the
spatio-temporal objects it contains.

(ii) Let us next consider briefly the possible bearing of the
results of psychical research on belief in immortality. There
have been those who have argued that here we have the best of
all empirical arguments for a future life. Even those like C. D.
Broad, who have been most cautious about the empirical phenomena, have nevertheless talked of the possible persistence of
some 'psychogenic factor', of some factor productive of 'mental
behaviour' at any rate over a limited period of time beyond
death.[1] Now I do not propose to examine these various claims
in detail. Nor is this the occasion to make a careful and critical
assessment of the facts.[2] But suppose it is the case (as seems very
likely) that after admitting what may be fraudulent, and what
may be given an alternative and not so exciting account, we
must nevertheless allow that some of the phenomena of some
seances and some accounts of poltergeists are veridical and
irreducible. What do we conclude?

The phenomena are significant in two ways.

(*a*) First, they are important in so far as they recreate for
many of our contemporaries a sense of wonder and mystery
when so much around us becomes more and more taped and
stereotyped; when so much of our behaviour becomes more and
more impersonal. The phenomena may be useful in reminding
us that the universe is a good deal odder and more mysterious
than many would like to think. Not for nothing is the spiritualist
Lyceum often to be found in that part of a sprawling city which
is most dismal and drab. When as infants we begin by drinking

[1] See e.g. *The Mind and its Place in Nature*, Ch. XII, and *An
Examination of McTaggart's Philosophy*, Cambridge, 1933, Vol. II,
Pt. II, Ch. LIV, esp. pp. 604f.

[2] Such as is done, for example, in G. N. M. Tyrrell, *The Personality
of Man*, Penguin Books, 1946, esp. Ch. IX and X. See also C. D. Broad,
Religion, Philosophy and Psychical Research, London, 1953, Section I,
Ch. I; R. C. Johnson, *Psychical Research* (Teach Yourself Books), 1959.

standard orange juice from a disinfected tumbler, and continue by taking up a medically approved straw our prescribed measure of milk from an artificially inseminated cow, thereafter having a full account of the physiology and psychology of sex, until at the end we are moved in composition caskets on ball-bearing rollers through synthetic curtains into electrically-heated furnaces – the movement being synchronized with a pre-recorded hymn – we may think that the time has come to give us all a numinous shudder or two. Let my argument not be mistaken. I am not being so silly and obscurantist as to condemn out of hand all social and scientific development. But I am saying that such developments do not easily provide intimations of immortality, and this fact is something with which empirical arguments for immortality need to reckon, as it is also something to which strange psychical phenomena provide a useful counterbalance.

(*b*) Secondly, the existence of abnormal psychical phenomena can usefully suggest that there is an element in personal intercourse beyond the observable behaviour with which we normally associate it. Even admitting that some spatio-temporal expression of personal activity is always necessary, abnormal psychical phenomena suggest that this element may in fact on occasion be supplied by someone else's body or (in the case of poltergeists) other physical phenomena altogether. This kind of possibility allows us a useful freedom in thinking about what constitutes, in terms of objects or spatio-temporal phenomena, personal behaviour. Further, this very freedom in relation to observables emphasises the point that characteristically personal behaviour is something which is more than the observables it displays, however diverse these be.

In short, the phenomena revealed and studied by psychical research can provide situations which reveal the transcendence of personal behaviour beyond its public and spatio-temporal manifestations. On the other hand, how this transcendence is best described is left problematical and we need not at all sponsor the kind of language about the 'spirit world' which spiritualists traditionally use to map their claims. Here is a point on which I will say something – if not very much – in my next chapter, where we shall be more explicitly concerned with the language in which claims for immortality are expressed.

(iii) We now pass to consider three other empirical arguments for immortality. First there is the argument from universal assent, what is traditionally called the argument *a consensu gentium*, which starts from the widespread popularity of the belief, noting that in various forms it has characterized many religions and many if not most civilisations. A second argument starts from the fact that it is very difficult, if not impossible, to think of our entire cessation. Even if we think of our Wills being read, we think of ourselves hovering round to see the look on old Uncle Sam's face when he hears that we have bequeathed to his reprobate brother that gold cigarette case he has long admired. A third argument tries to develop the alleged analogy between sleep and spring on the one hand, and death on the other: as we wake from sleep, or as spring follows winter, so (it has been argued) we shall survive death.

Once again, to mention such arguments is to provoke counter-arguments. With regard to the first argument, there is the irrefutable fact that even eight million people might be wrong. Why should we perpetuate the Election Fallacy and suppose that what the majority believe, is for that reason necessarily correct? Again, to turn to the second argument, the very act of imagining ourselves present at the reading of our Will, inevitably puts us into the picture. We cannot expect to imagine ourselves present anywhere without having to suppose that we are in some way there, if only peeping from the side-wings. As for the third argument based on the alleged analogy between death and spring or sleep, the analogy, it is said, is quite worthless. It is the obvious differences, not the superficial similarities, between a dead person and someone sleeping, which are significant and important, and there are easy and reliable tests by which to distinguish a dead tree from a tree in winter, despite again their superficial resemblances.

But at this point the pendulum of the argument begins to

82

swing the other way. An error that was committed by (say) eight thousand million people of such diverse creeds and civilisations, would – even as an error – be a curious fact; especially since the existence of the original belief could easily and alternatively be accounted for by supposing that for most people, at one time or another, there occur situations which reveal them, at least to themselves, as more than the public behaviour they display.

Again, with the second argument in mind, it might be said that the important reason why we find it difficult to think of ourselves in the future as 'not there' is precisely because we already recognise, as we have said, certain situations which here and now are not exhausted by our present public behaviour. This is the reason, it would be said, why we are not tempted to conclude that the disappearance of our public behaviour to-morrow will mean the end of 'us' *altogether*. For it does not mean the whole of 'us' today. We can mutter with Spinoza – even if out of its context – *'sentimus experimurque nos aeternos esse'*[1]: 'we discern and discover that we are eternal'. We can claim with Butler that to recognise 'ourselves' is to recognise 'ourselves' as more than 'gross bodies'.[2]

The argument from considerations about sleeping or winter needs a little more attention. As an argument by analogy, any argument comparing the transition from winter to spring with the transition from death to subsequent life, is plainly weak and confused. It is virtually worthless. But suppose that the argument, the story, the talk, has a different logical point altogether. In the first place, let the argument first suggest to us that we ponder the contrast of winter and spring. What happens? Quite apart from what the botanist or gardener may tell us, we look on a winter's scene and everything is drab, lifeless, bleak and impersonal. We are numb and inactive with cold. We even say our feet are 'dead'. Then comes spring, and the lifeless begins to show life: buds and blossom appear. Green replaces black. Everywhere the scene changes and in every detail. We even

[1] Spinoza, *Ethic*, Bk. V, Prop. XXIII, Scholium.
[2] J. Butler, *The Analogy*, Conclusion to Part I.

speak of nature 'coming alive'. At this point let us recall that few circumstances are better than change for reminding us of what abides; witness the easy way by which days registering change, such as New Year's Day, birthdays, anniversary days, and the rest, take on a religious significance. Further, when people are moved by the beauty of blossom and spring flowers, they often talk about 'empathy', that curious feeling or sense of kinship with something other than ourselves – that *Einfühlung* – that which (it is said) characterises an aesthetic situation. So to make a contrast between winter and spring is likely to be a successful technique by which to evoke a characteristically religious situation, one in which we discern what abides in what changes, what is seen *and more*.

The second stage of the argument takes this contrast between winter and spring and brings it, as a sort of catalyst, alongside a case of death. Someone is lying dead. Superficially (or so we would say) nothing is left but this dead body. But if we bring alongside the contrast between winter and spring, there is at least enough resemblance (despite major differences) between winter and death for an interlocking of pictures, whereupon a situation is evoked around the dead body as it was earlier evoked by the winter-spring contrast alone. Like manganese dioxide, which as a catalyst assists enormously in the evolution of oxygen from potassium chlorate, without itself being directly involved[1] in the chemical reaction, the winter-spring contrast accelerates and brings off (as we might say) the larger evocation, and without being necessarily involved in the phenomena of death – as it would be if we linked it by the logical relations of an argument from analogy. It is as though (to change the metaphor) having once seen some junior archdeacon 'come alive'[2] when he exchanges cassock apron and gaiters for linen apron and dishcloth, one can then see even the most prelatical-looking bishop as 'having a human heart'.[2]

[1] Or so the elementary theory of catalysts has it.

[2] And the inverted commas remind us that these phrases have to be used curiously – and not as scientifically descriptive – to make their point.

Once there has been in this way and around the phenomena of death, a situation not restricted to the dead body and other phenomena which it undoubtedly contains, then we are able to 'see' that the physical accompaniments of death, the cessation of a certain kind of objective behaviour, no more exhaust a dead person's existence than the contrast between winter and spring leave us unmoved. Needless to say, if the original contrast *does* leave us unmoved, the 'argument' has from the beginning no hope of being successful. Nor is it *bound* to succeed even if the original contrast is in itself evocative. For various reasons, there may be no catalytic interlocking. We may, for instance, as a matter of psychological fact, be so impressed by the differences between winter and death that no similarity whatever is recognised. The prelate may be so prelatical that *all* similarities to the archdeacon disappear.

Take now the story of sleeping. Here, too, the argument cannot start by saying that sleeping is like death. Once again, it is rather that the contrast between ourselves as sleeping and ourselves as waking can be used to evoke a 'more than objects' situation which in its turn can be used to assure us that death never exhausts our total existence. Whether with the transition of sleeping-waking, or that of winter-spring, the contrast can be used to evoke and reveal the kind of situation in which immortality is grounded.

In the case of sleeping, however, we may express our point in another way altogether. We may recognise that to make a straight comparison between sleeping and dying can never be the basis of a good argument, because such a comparison ignores obvious and important differences between the two states. Even so, despite these differences, 'I am asleep' has certain similarities to 'I am dead'. Neither can be significantly uttered by the subject of the assertions: though at the same time there is no difficulty about someone else's saying of me either, 'He is asleep', or 'He is dead'. With these last two assertions there is no logical or empirical embarrassment whatever. Now, why is it that one pair of assertions – 'I'm asleep' and 'I'm dead' – is problematical whereas the other pair – 'He's asleep' and 'He's dead' – is not? The reason, I suggest, is that 'dead' and 'asleep' are amongst the very few words in our language whose meaning is inevitably and most plainly given in terms of objects. They therefore attach themselves naturally and appropriately to 'He' – a person as objectified for everyone to see. So we have no difficulty over 'He is dead' and 'He is asleep'. Each is logically homogeneous, and none of the words needs relate to more than objects. But the case is different when we introduce the word 'I'. Here is a word which cannot be wholly 'public', which relates to 'objects' and more. So it happens that when such words as 'dead' and 'asleep' are joined with the word 'I', logical oddities, hybrids, are produced such as 'I am asleep' and 'I am dead'.

At this point it may be countered that all that is odd about these assertions arises from the fact that people who are dead and people who are asleep do not talk, and that there is no more to the oddness than this. That there *is* this difficulty we need not deny. That one of the problems about asserting 'I am dead' is that we do not talk when we are dead, must obviously be granted. But the difficulty isn't merely that I cannot *say*, for example, 'I am dead'; it is that, while I cannot say 'I am dead', there is no difficulty whatever about someone else saying of me 'He is dead'. So there is at any rate the possibility that these two sentences do not talk about precisely the same kind of situation.

Let me put my point another way. Normally, we suppose that 'I'm eating' describes a situation identical with what an observer describes as 'He's eating'; or 'I'm running' a situation identical with what is described by 'He's running', and so on. And the supposition works normally so well that philosophers such as Hume can be found who have endeavoured to argue logical identity between the two classes of assertion. On this view, 'I' and 'he' are logically interchangeable, so that 'I' relates to no more than 'he' legitimately describes, i.e. to a series of 'objects' or observables, what the eighteenth century called 'ideas', what nowadays would be called my 'public behaviour'.

But what the puzzle of 'I am asleep' and 'I am dead' does, I

86

would say, is to cast doubts on the logical assimilation which such a one as Hume would have us make. Indeed, those who would say that the difficulty is no more than that dead men and sleeping men do not talk, by saying that, in fact reveal their hand. For they are now saying by implication that in principle 'I' am no more than a talker, i.e. no more than my public behaviour. On such a view the *only* difficulty about 'I am dead' is that on any occasion when it serves to be said, there is no talker to utter it. Whereas I have suggested that there is a *further* difficulty – the mixed character of what is logically a hybrid.

It follows of course that when *I myself* talk of my 'running' or my 'eating', these words *for me* mean 'more' than what any observer can describe: otherwise we would have countless logical hybrids throughout the whole of our language. But this view – that a first person singular activity word tells of more than 'objects' – makes no new claim. It is wholly consistent with what was said in Chapters I and II about free will – that my 'free' activity is more than the public behaviour which expresses it.

There is perhaps yet another point worth making. Suppose someone says: 'I am asleep' or 'I am dead'. These are assertions which would be falsified on utterance. We may now remark how similar they therefore are to the *cogito* of Descartes. Here again, the very utterance of the doubt, 'I am not existing', is enough to falsify it.

Now, as G. E. Moore pointed out in lectures some twenty-five years ago,[1] the *cogito* of Descartes might be compared with the assertion – 'I am not saying the word "cat".' This is equally well falsified on utterance. The logical behaviour of all these assertions is therefore (i) quite unlike that of any straightforward empirical assertions, such, for example, as 'The elephant is not pink', or 'Stanley did not say "Dr Livingstone, I presume".' Nor (ii) are any of the earlier assertions false on inspection, like a formal contradiction such as 'p and not-p'. They are therefore logical peculiars, and I suggest that their peculiarity arises from

[1] I do not, of course, father on Moore the application I am making of his remark.

the fact that they are special assertions about my own activity whose point is to reveal that I myself and my own activity is something more than the public behaviour I exhibit. Who is to tell whether 'I' am 'actually' saying the word 'cat' or not? Is the occurrence of the noise 'cat' from my mouth an infallible clue?

But have these reflections taken us too far? Is it *ever* possible then to give *any* account of 'I am dead'? Is there *any* way of understanding such a sentence? Can we, in short, do anything to overcome the difficulties which arise from the fact that while 'I' is not exhausted by object words, 'dead', as we normally use the word, is? To answer those questions let us return to our starting point,[1] for we have plainly come back very close to it. Let us begin by taking 'dead' as no more than a descriptive word equivalent to 'mortality'. The picture this calls up is of all our public behaviour coming gradually to an end – whether biochemical, psychological, sociological, and the rest. We reflect . . . yes, the day will come when, in my case, there is that final breakdown of organic processes, that permanent failure of appropriate behaviour responses, that ultimate cessation of the social round, that pay-out of premiums, that visit of the undertaker. Suppose in this way we begin to pare off from our existence all the features that the descriptive word 'dead' covers, whereupon our lives become empirically less and less and less. What is the outcome?

As is well known, some become mad, terror-stricken. They are then said to be 'beside themselves' or 'out of their mind'. Nor is this surprising. Because for them, and in their case, 'I' has disappeared. They never were more than could have been known with complete satisfaction by the competent and skilled biologist, psychologist, social worker, economist, and so on. Yet with others the case is utterly different. For these, the same kind of sequence may lead them to talk in terms of such phrases as 'peace', 'Nirvana', 'eternal life in Christ Jesus', and so on. What has happened in this second case? Our suggestion is that these phrases, whatever differences they might have between

[1] See pp. 64ff.

them, have at any rate this important similarity, that they are all used as appropriate currency when the story we have just told, or some similar one,[1] has led at some point or another to a disclosure, a disclosure of my existence as something more than the most skilled and competent external observer could give an account of. To use such phrases as I have just listed is thus to acknowledge that even stories of death can bring intimations of immortality. Even talk about death may evoke the kind of situation which it has been my purpose throughout this chapter, as well as in other chapters, to emphasise. We may even say, summarily, that whether or not we believe in immortality depends on the meaning which 'I am dead' has for us.[2]

In this chapter, then, I have tried to show that the justification of immortality will depend on whether our behaviour can be exhaustively described in spatio-temporal terms or not. If the life of a person is no more than the behaviour pattern he exhibits, there is no sense in talking of im-mortality; if human 'life' is no more than its public expression, there is certainly no meaning in the phrase ' "life" after death'. For death brings our publicity to an end, and makes our 'mortality' complete. Further, we have seen that the arguments and counter-arguments for immortality are all concerned to substantiate or deny this central claim – that personal behaviour is not exhausted by all that object language talks of. We are immortal in so far as we know a situation which transcends space and time. How far traditional language about immortality can do justice to such an empirical grounding of the concept we shall see in our next chapter.

Meanwhile, let me emphasise that my purpose has not been to give a full account of the arguments and counter-arguments which have traditionally characterised discourse about immortality. Much more would need to be said if that were so. My purpose has rather been to display what I consider to be the crucial point which is at issue between these arguments and

[1] E.g. that of the Four Noble Truths and the Eight-fold Path, for the Buddhist.

[2] Cp. W. H. Poteat, 'I will die: an analysis', *Philosophical Quarterly*, Vol. 9, No. 34, Jan. 1959, pp. 46-58.

counter-arguments, and it is this: that whether or not we believe in immortality depends on whether or not we admit a certain kind of situation which the one kind of argument tries to deny and atrophy, and the other kind of argument claims and tries to evoke.

IV

LANGUAGE ABOUT IMMORTALITY: ETERNAL LIFE AND THE SOUL

WHAT SITUATION justifies belief in immortality? The answer we gave in the previous chapter was in effect: Any situation which, subjectively, is my public behaviour and more. In particular, situations of 'freedom' offer us at one and the same time discernments of immortality as well. When we are 'free', when we exhibit what we called 'personal decision', we are 'alive' in a sense which mortality cannot exhaust; half-decided, we are half-alive – wholly 'official', and from the standpoint of 'personality' we are dead already. So it happens that the point of arguments and counter-arguments which have traditionally characterised discussions of immortality has been, all details aside, to claim or deny respectively that personal behaviour is not exhausted by what object language treats of. Finally, we saw that 'I am asleep' and 'I am dead' are logical conundrums which arise from the fact that 'asleep' and 'dead' are amongst the very few words we use which are necessarily public in their unpacking, so that 'I am asleep' and 'I am dead' are logical hybrids, mixing words which differ enormously in their logical behaviour. The very existence of the puzzle indeed witnesses to the fact that 'I', *unlike* 'asleep' and 'dead', cannot be restricted to what is spatio-temporal. There is, therefore, no sense in talking of 'I' as such coming to an end. All such temporal characterisations as 'ending' must relate to my public behaviour, to 'me'.

Again, if persons were 'objects', and since death means the

end of all public behaviour, 'life' (in this sense) 'after death' for *such* 'persons' would certainly be meaningless. But because 'persons' are objects *and more*, even if death means the end of public behaviour, the existence of 'persons' after death can still be significantly spoken of. But how is it rightly to be talked about? If a word like 'immortality' has to have such logical behaviour as anchors it firmly into the kind of situation we have been trying to evoke throughout this book, what kind of logical behaviour will this be? Further, what logical structure has to be given to such phrases as 'unending life', 'everlasting life', 'timeless self', and so on, if these are to be given similar anchorages? These and similar questions will be our concern in this chapter.

Our first task will be to show that the words and phrases we have just quoted are best understood in terms of what I have called 'qualified models'.[1] It is convenient to take 'immortality' first, because our discussion of this word can incorporate some of the reflections with which I concluded the previous chapter.

As we shall see, the logical structure of 'immortality' is best represented by dividing the word into two and re-writing it: 'im-mortality'. In such a phrase, 'mortality' specifies what we have called a model, circumstances which we can readily understand. 'Im' as a qualifier develops this model in a characteristic way, a way we have already in fact outlined in the last chapter. We begin (as we did there) with the model 'mortality', which specifies (say) the biological, psychological and social features of death. The function of the prefix 'im' is then operational. Like the square root sign in mathematics, it directs us to *do* something. We do not look for its 'meaning' as though it referred to some great Nothing. It works as an operator, and as an operator it directs us to press on with the mortality story, to develop it ever further and further. At each point in the story, no matter how far the story has been developed, the operator has the effect of whispering in our ear, 'Not just this'; 'This isn't

[1] Cp. p. 47 above.

enough': 'This is an inadequate account.' Whereupon our immediate reaction is to press the organic, biochemical, psychological and social stories ever further; to specify such features of 'mortality' or 'death' in even greater and more complex detail. In this way, at each point of the story 'im' registers our dissatisfaction with the story to date, as an adequate account of 'ourselves', and the story is consequentially developed yet further in an endeavour to satisfy. Nor will there be any limit to such development. For, to recall the general point about infinite divisibility and expansibility made at the start of the first chapter (and quite apart from all other subsequent considerations) no situation at any given time will ever be exhaustively covered by object language.[1] Yet object language is what the language of mortality inevitably is. So we go on and on, and our hope is that there will break in on us, at some point or other, a disclosure in which we see that we are more than all the objective features we have enumerated or could ever enumerate. The story is developed until the fact that we are more than organic processes, biochemical changes, behaviour responses, premium holders, etc. becomes evident. The disclosure, as it occurs, takes into itself any and every such object feature.

If we want an illustration to help us to see better what all this comes to, to help us to see how a story about 'objects' can be developed so as to effect a disclosure, let us consider a small child's drawing-book, where one page is covered in large measure with dots. I am thinking of those long sequences of dots which the small child is instructed to join in order to make the outline of some picture. Suppose that, instead of putting lines between the dots, when presented with some particular picture, we put other dots between the dots as originally given, so developing the 'object' story. Even so, at this first move, we may still not 'see' anything clearly. The next move will then be to put still more dots between the new dots and the old, and after this we may yet put further dots between these dots and the earlier dots, and so on. It may be, if we are all very stupid,

[1] See pp. 15-17 above.

that even then we do not recognise what the drawing is meant to be; it may even be that no matter how many dots we insert, the picture does not break in on us, and there is no disclosure. On the other hand, at some stage or another we may suddenly say, 'By jove, it is a cock perching on a farmyard midden with a tractor standing behind', and in saying that, we should have shown that we had absorbed all the dots we had drawn, and all the dots anyone could ever draw. In a similar way we develop the story of 'death' or 'mortality' in terms of an ever-increasing number of 'objects', in terms of ever more detailed organic, biochemical, psychological, economic stories, until what we are – all this objective behaviour *and more* – dawns on us, and we 'see' ourselves as 'immortal'.

To revert now to our exposition – here we may say is a sort of negative approach to the concept of immortality comparable to the way in which we might evoke a situation to justify the word 'God' by using phrases of negative theology like 'immutable', 'impassible', 'uncreate', or even 'without body, parts or passions'.[1] We may next note that the same kind of logical structure might be given to the expression 'unending life', which would then be read as 'un ending-life', or to the expression 'endless life' which would then be read as '*not* life-with-an-end'. In such expressions the phrases 'ending-life' or 'life-with-an-end' would call up the kind of account of the end of life which, as we have seen, is supplied by biology, psychology, sociology and so on. But at each and every such account of 'ending-life', at each and every particular version of 'life-with-an-end', the prefix 'un' or 'not' would register our permanent dissatisfaction. And so the story would develop until, as we might hope, a disclosure was evoked to give the foundation 'in fact' for the phrase with which we started.

On the other hand, 'unending life' or 'endless life' might be given a somewhat different structure, though one which conforms to the same logical scheme. We might take 'unending life' or 'endless life' as equivalent to 'everlasting life', 'life-

[1] For more details see my *Religious Language*, pp. 50-53.

without any end', 'life – for ever and ever'.[1] The difference between this second structure and our earlier account is this. Whereas our qualifiers, so far, have been negative in their approach, here is one which is positive. When we take 'unending' or 'endless' as equivalent to 'everlasting' or 'ever and ever', the qualifier is no longer 'un' but 'unending'. We now begin not with the model of 'ending life', but with 'life' as such. What models does the word 'life' now call up? There are the occasions when we are only 'half alive'; other occasions when we are 'very much alive' and bubbling over with 'vitality'. There is the vitality of the business tycoon at whose behest telephones ring and teleprinters knock. Or we think of the vitality of the orator who addresses a crowd of one hundred thousand in some great stadium, or audience of millions over a radio and television network. But even the longest oration comes to an end – the orator takes off his boots and puts his feet up; and the executive in due course makes room for another. Whereupon we may reflect that the vitality of some 'village Hampden', while in obvious ways comparatively restricted, may nevertheless be expressed over almost a lifetime of dutiful service. In one way or another, then, the extent to which a man's influence spreads over time is a measure of his vitality. What, now, if this spread is quite unlimited, quite unrestricted? What of the life whose temporal spread is never completed, but which is ever greater and greater in its extent? So the story would develop until it brought about the disclosure it was designed to effect. And when the disclosure occurred we should know what 'unending' or 'everlasting' 'life' is contriving to talk about; we would know 'vitality' indeed. For there will have broken in on us that 'more-than-object' situation to which these words and phrases rightly belong.

Associating this last example with its predecessor it is interesting to notice that if we now take the word 'eternal' as a

[1] In this form the phrases are obviously similar to the phrase 'future life', but as we shall show in the next chapter, that phrase may also have its own peculiar complex logical setting, and is best treated separately.

qualifier it can work in both ways: both negatively and positively, when it operates on 'life' (i.e. observable behaviour) as a model. In the first way, 'eternal' would remind us: 'temporal features are not the whole story'. Attached to 'life', where 'life' is modelled in terms of public behaviour, the operator 'eternal' would constantly direct our attention *beyond and away from* all its temporal features in an endeavour to help us discern what abides, and 'eternal life' would now have a logical behaviour like 'im-mortality', 'un-ending life' and 'not life-with-an-end'.

Alternatively, 'eternal' could direct us to pass beyond the spatio-temporal, *but* this time while *including* it. Working with this interpretation of the qualifier 'eternal', we would readily acknowledge and now incorporate into our story this, that and every feature of a man's life. Nothing would be excluded. We would be avaricious for the latest facts dropping hot from the biochemist's or psychiatrist's oven. Our eagerness to incorporate any and every acknowledged fact would be equalled only by our stout refusal to take any description to date as adequate. A man's 'life', we would say, 'consisteth not in the abundance of the things which he possesseth', though what those things are, and what a man does with them, may well lead us to see in what this 'life' does in fact consist. Undoubtedly there is a 'life'[1] and a 'richness' to be talked of in terms of bigger and bigger harvests filling greater and greater barns. But whether a man is 'rich' beyond this – significantly spoken of (let us notice) as 'rich toward God' – depends on whether a man is not only a prosperous farmer but more as well. It is the function of the word 'eternal' to direct us to a recognition of this 'more'. 'Eternal' would now be moving us towards a recognition of what is to break in on us as we survey more and more of the public behaviour which can characterize a man. Here would be 'life *indeed*', 'life abundant *and eternal*', and the italicized words witness to a disclosure which embracing abundance goes also

[1] 'Soul (=life), thou hast much goods laid up for many years' (Luke 12.19).

96

beyond it. 'Eternal life' now works like 'everlasting life' in the second illustration above.

We can thus see how phrases such as 'immortality', 'unending life', 'everlasting life', 'eternal life', can become appropriate currency for the situation which is in each case the empirical anchorage. If we had somehow to choose between these phrases, a provisional conclusion might express a preference for 'eternal life', at any rate in so far as this phrase embodies in itself two possible logical structures, either of which can lead us to the situation in whose occurrence will be found the meaning that they all contrive to express.

Let us look next at the phrases 'timeless self' and 'pure ego'. I suggest here again we regard them as qualified models. On this interpretation we take as our model the 'self' or the 'ego', meaning by these words that which is public about me to everybody including myself – what everyone, including myself, can readily agree about me. 'Timeless' and 'pure' are both of them qualifiers for such a model, urging us so to talk about our temporal characteristics and public behaviour as to make more evident – in a disclosure – 'what is the case' besides. The directive now is to call up all our temporal characteristics only to dismiss them, and to play this game of constant rejection until there breaks in on us what we are more than our observable behaviour.[1]

But this suggests a further point of interest and importance. Plainly the exercise we have just outlined for understanding a phrase such as 'timeless self' is something which each of us performs best in his own case. Yet I would most certainly wish to go further and to say that in the case of other persons we could, in principle, use the phrase 'timeless self' of them with the same kind of empirical justification. It would then be based on our awareness of what in *their* case they are besides their public behaviour.

This would be established by our surveying this and that

[1] Descartes' methodological doubt is an example of this technique. See *Discourse on Method*, esp. Pt. IV, and *Meditations*, esp. I and II.

feature of their public behaviour until a disclosure situation occurred around such features as we had to date enumerated. In such a case we should not only see Alciphron[1] in the sense of seeing Alciphron's hair, skin, eyes, and so on. We should now 'see' Alciphron himself. Alciphron as a 'person', Alciphron as a 'timeless self', Alciphron as 'immortal'. The oculist sees Jean when he looks at her eyes. But what has happened when the oculist looks 'into' (not at) Jean's eyes? What has happened when we say on such an occasion that, e.g. he now sees Jean as a 'person'; and the 'real' Jean now confronts him? The answer is that around Jean's eyes has been evoked a situation transcending the spatio-temporal, a situation by reference to which our use of the phrase 'timeless self' of Jean is justified.

In any event, in this context of immortality or eternal life, do not let us make a mistake of which our discussion of free will has forewarned us. Do not let us suppose that the situation in which 'immortality' or 'eternal life' are grounded is somehow 'purely subjective'; so that, when we reach an awareness of ourselves as immortal, it is of ourselves in some sort of independent and isolated existence. It is true that when the disclosure occurs in our own case, it will be *our* transcendence of the spatio-temporal; *our* reach beyond public behaviour; *our* immortality of which we become aware. But more will be disclosed than that. There will be some objective reference to reckon with.

It was, I think, one of the greatest mistakes of the Absolute Idealist, and not least of F. H. Bradley, to suppose that when situations such as we have been stressing throughout this book were evoked,[2] they were, so to say, structurally homogeneous, that in such situations the distinction between subject and object disappeared. The Absolute could only too easily be regarded as a Night in which every cow – and everything else for that matter – was uniformly black. Admittedly, when a

[1] To take Bishop Berkeley's character in the Dialogues known by that title, and when he makes a similar point – *Alciphron*, Dial. IV. 5.

[2] And he gives an excellent account of their evocation in his *Essays on Truth and Reality*, Oxford, 1914, Ch. VI: 'Immediate Experience'.

disclosure-situation is evoked, we have gone beyond and transcended 'objects' if an 'object' means what public language talks
of. But we have *not* gone beyond any and all 'objectivity' altogether. For in being aware of ourselves as 'transcending' our
public behaviour, we are also aware of some 'transcendent'
Other as well, which is likewise 'transcendent' in being more
than what public language speaks of. Nor is this any very novel
or revolutionary doctrine. It follows at once from recognizing
that no experience we have, not even that of our 'immortality',
can be utterly subjective; or, if we wish to express the point
another way, if ever there were any purely subjective experience
it would be beyond our ken and beyond our language to talk of it.

Just as with every conviction of freedom there goes an
awareness of some obligation, just as freedom is a response to
obligation; so with our conviction about our own immortality,
there goes an awareness of some Other which – like ourselves –
is not restricted to the spatio-temporal. With awareness of our
own immortality there goes an awareness of what some, like
McTaggart, have called 'other persons', or what others, like the
later Hebrews, have called 'other persons and God'.[1] In either
case, and this brings us back to the remark which introduced
this digression, 'persons' as transcending the spatio-temporal
are 'immortal' like ourselves, and if we go further and speak of
'God' as well, we rightly and not unexpectedly, bring alongside
a word like 'eternal' as a logical kinsman.

We have now seen the kind of logical structure to be given
to such phrases as 'immortality', 'eternal life', 'everlasting life',
'pure ego' and 'timeless self'. We have seen the kind of logical

---

[1] This is the broad philosophical base to such more detailed
theological assertions as the following:
Dan. 7.18, 27: 'But the saints of the Most High shall receive the
kingdom, and possess the kingdom for ever, even for ever and ever. . . .
But the kingdom and the dominion . . . shall be given to the people of
the saints of the Most High: his kingdom is an everlasting kingdom,
and all dominions shall serve and obey him.' Wisd. 3.1, 4, 8, 9: 'The
souls of the righteous are in the hand of God . . . their hope is full of
immortality . . . the Lord shall reign over them for evermore . . . they
that are faithful through love shall abide with him' (RV and margin).

behaviour they exhibit, and the kind of empirical situation in which they can be anchored. To complete this chapter let us look in some detail at one more basic concept, viz. that of the soul. If we have justified belief in immortality, have we also justified belief in what is called the Immortality of the Soul? In answer to the question, 'What is immortal?' would we answer, 'the soul'?

Let us first recall that any situation which justifies talk about 'immortality' is also one of those by reference to which the full use of the word 'I' will alone be given. So we shall make no logical misallocations, we shall mislead neither ourselves nor anyone else, if we speak not so much of the 'immortality of the soul' as of the 'immortality of I' or of 'my immortality'. It is true that 'I', in referring to what is distinctively personal about a certain situation, also refers to my public behaviour as well, and some might think that this is an unfortunate implication. But when we speak of the 'immortality of I' we not only and obviously do *not* imply the permanent persistence of this or that particular body which on such and such an occasion now exposes 'I' to my contemporaries. Such a particular occasion, once it has occurred, vanishes for ever. On the other hand, the great merit of talking of the 'immortality of I' is that it emphasises that our immortality is founded in a situation of that distinctive kind which now justifies us in our distinctive use of 'I'. So our first conclusion is that if we are asked, 'What is immortal?', 'I' is the best answer we can give,[1] since it is a word which quite emphatically has for its cash-value more than our public behaviour. Contrariwise, it would not be so much false as logically inept and grossly misleading to speak of the 'immortality of NWPC/163/2', or the 'immortality of the mayor', or the 'immortality of the booking clerk'.

What, then, of 'the immortality of the soul'? Plainly the phrase is dangerously like those we have just criticised, and the case is not improved when it is further assimilated by some

---

[1] We shall see later that significantly for the Hebrews, 'immortality of the soul' = the 'immortality of "I"'. (pp. 110ff).

users to 'the long life of my *Exide* battery' which (so the advertisements tell us) 'still keeps going when the rest have stopped'. For here some property – 'long life' – is being predicated of a 'thing' or an 'object' – an accumulator – and we have an assertion about nothing but 'observables'. Yet we shall clearly deny the very claim we are most anxious to make – we shall by our own words give the lie to our own utterance – if we allow it to be supposed that in a parallel sort of way 'immortality' is ever the 'property' of some 'thing' or 'object' called the 'soul'. To use the word 'soul' in such a way would be logically irresponsible and cavalier. If, of course, anyone wished to use the word 'soul' just to designate what there is in that distinctive situation which a word like 'immortality' evokes, besides the public behaviour it contains, then I would have no grumble, and that is a point we take up in the next section.[1] But we would still have left on our hands the logical behaviour of this word 'soul', and the danger will always be that we will start to use 'soul' as though it described an object. The danger will always be that, quite uninhibited by logical after-thoughts, we shall start talking with cheerful frequency about the 'soul' as if a soul had a status which was quite parallel to that of scientific objects.

Consider, by way of example, those who were called Traducianists, some of whom affirmed that the soul was a product of the generative powers of man. Others then tried to avoid the obvious conclusion that the soul is something like a biological organism by saying that while parents generate a sensitive soul, God changes this into a spiritual one. But this piece of verbal embroidery was never more than a pleasing jingle calculated to give momentary cheer, and in due course the organic picture came very much into its own again when some wished to argue that each man's soul was tainted, discoloured, infected at birth. Nor was there lack of logical circumspection on one side only. On the other side the Creationists, who held that each soul was a creation of God, could talk of this soul being 'infused' into the body chosen for it. We may well wonder what all this comes

[1] See p. 105.

to. What is being claimed? What is being talked of by using the word 'infused'? How often have theological theories been formulated in this way without regard for their logical complexity? How often have theological problems been discussed like this as though they were problems of a scientific character which on principle they obviously cannot be?

It is when such mistakes are made that there can easily arise a theology without religion, theological terms devoid of any religious reference, controversies which are mere word-spinning, discussions about the soul, which may provide verbal exercise for those with nothing better to do, but are otherwise utterly pointless. Nor are the dangers narrowly theological. For to parallel talk of the soul with talk of physical objects is, as we have already seen, to invite an account of the soul in no more than biological, psychological, or behaviouristic terms. Further, it also makes it rather too easy in our own day for moral evil to be set aside as some psychological aberration, for sin to be excused as some psychical abnormality.

Nor, presented with these various difficulties, must we then do a double-think and make the soul something quite isolated, all by itself, in some isolated theological world. For we shall then have escaped one problem only to find an even more insuperable one in its place. We shall have a soul secure and sacrosanct right enough, but permitting of no intelligible assertion whatever about it. Nay further, the chances are that before very long we shall forget this theological isolation, and without any logical qualms revert to old ways of talking. Nor, if we realise what we are doing, can we then defend this merely by talking of sublime paradox or deep mystery. For to talk of the soul as if it were some special kind of physical object, yet in the same breath to deny it is a physical object, is neither sublime paradox nor deep mystery; it is sheer inconsistency and shallow confusion. If we wish to maintain the theological distinctiveness of the soul, we must at least give some sort of hint as to the kind of logical peculiarity which soul-language exhibits. How often has such a hint been lacking!

Take, for instance, S. Baring-Gould's hymn.[1] Like all hymns, it *may* receive its necessary logical qualifications from the contextual setting – the worship in which it normally occurs. But, as it stands, it bristles with possible misunderstandings. Take only the following lines:

> On the Resurrection morning
>   Soul and body meet again.

Meanwhile . . .

> The soul in contemplation
>   Utters earnest prayer and strong,
> Bursting at the Resurrection
>   Into song.

Is a 'soul' something which can meet a 'body'? Further, is the soul which is this isolated entity, something which can burst into song? At the same time, let it be allowed in fairness that somehow to relate the word 'soul' to contemplation and prayer is wise and proper. Nor would I like to suggest that this hymn is either the only or the worst possible example of illegitimate logical placing. The same could be said for much theological controversy, and not only about the soul, that has not been circumspect about the logical geography of its concepts. But too much theology – whether expert like Traducianism, or popular like this hymn – has used language in blatant disregard of its peculiar logical structure. It has used language which, misleading its users and hearers alike, can make unbelievers of us all.

Similar reflections are possible with regard to the phrase 'timeless self', which from one point of view might be regarded as a logical synonym for 'immortal soul'. We have *not* to associate the *logical* behaviour of 'timeless self' with that of grammatical kinsmen such as 'better self' or 'off-duty self'. It does not describe a distinctive kind of public existence in the way in which these latter phrases do. It is not, for instance, to

[1] *The English Hymnal*, 136.

be paralleled with what the mayor's wife may call her husband's 'parlour self', or the bishop's wife may call her husband's 'purple self'. There have been many misunderstandings, some popular and some sophisticated, which have arisen from such mistaken logical assimilations as these, from a failure to give to phrases such as 'immortality' and 'timeless self' their appropriately odd logical structure. We cannot too often emphasise that such phrases will only be justified when they are anchored in a disclosure-situation as and when evoked. In short, 'immortality' and 'unending life' do not tell of some 'property' of a 'thing' called the soul, or of some existence like our public behaviour now, but going on and on and on. They tell rather of a situation we know *now* which is characteristically distinctive in being more than spatio-temporal. So I am certainly not arguing for any 'thing' which would be called the 'soul', something thought of as a special kind of 'me' existing in some shadowy realm. If we ask 'What is immortal?' the most helpful answer we can give is 'I'. But, it may be said, am I then proposing immortality without souls, and immortality without a future life?

To take up the challenge of that question we must now say something more about souls, and in the next chapter we shall offer some suggestions about the kind of logical structure which belongs to the more complex doctrines of a future life. If the reader is with me so far, let him agree, at least for the sake of argument, that immortality relates to a situation which trans-cends public behaviour, which is spatio-temporal events *and more*. The major problem with which we are then left, and the problem which has been so sharply raised by what we have said about the logical misreading of familiar phrases, is this: How then are we to talk, in an extended sort of way, about that which, in a discernment of our immortality, transcends public be-haviour? What account can we give of that extensively developed kind of language which has been traditionally used about *the more*? We shall conclude this chapter (as I have said) with some further sketching of the logical geography of the word 'soul', reserving for the next chapter a consideration of all those doctrines of immortality which cluster around the concept of a 'future life'.

We have already noticed that traditional doctrines of immortality have often developed language about the soul which has been a logical duplicate of language about physical objects. We have had a man's soul as a shadowy existent, some kind of counterpart of this body, and when 'spirit' has been used as a synonym for 'soul' we have had spirits indulging in the most extraordinary kind of activities. If the huntsman's 'spirit' has not been out with the spiritual hounds, it has been riding again with the huntsman's earthly successors as an invisible companion; the spirit of some medical genius in the past has been giving help to the inexperienced Registrar as he nervously treads the ward floor, or has been helping the medically unqualified to bring off spectacular cures. Here is duplicate language of the most misleading kind.

But, as we have already admitted[1] we must not over-argue the point; we must not suppose that this kind of language, logically misleading though it be, is *utterly* bogus. Let us not conclude that it talks about nothing because it talks of what could not possibly be bodies, i.e. spirits, in what is duplicate of body language. Even if we are rightly critical (as we have been) of such duplicate language and its misleading pictures, let us not conclude that it can be wholly cast aside without the least loss. Extravagant though the language be, it has a respectable basis of which we should never lose sight, and which it is worth continually emphasising.

Let us see, and first by an example which is somewhat remote from theology, that while we do well to reject the extravagances, we shall nevertheless err if we conclude that those who perpetrate them are talking about nothing. In fact they are only making bad attempts to talk about something, whose correct currency thus remains an open question and possibility.[2] The

[1] See p. 101.
[2] This may even be the case with Traducianism, and Creationism which we mentioned above, p. 101.

non-theological example we shall give to illustrate this counsel of caution, concerns universals. Suppose we see a yellow flower, a yellow light, a yellow dress, a yellow hat, a banana and so on. Suppose again we see a good deed here, there and everywhere. There may then be evoked, by means of such a sequence, a disclosure-situation such as we have been emphasising throughout this book. Now I suggest that it is when a sequence of yellow objects or a sequence of good deeds has effected a disclosure and a discernment, that people have begun to speak of 'Yellow' – of yellow with a capital y – or (say) of 'eternal yellowness', of Good, or 'eternal goodness'. But because we can and would give such words and phrases this kind of reputable and reliable foundation, it does *not* justify us in talking of Goodness and Yellowness as if they were 'things' laid up in some heavenly region as paint might be laid up on a shelf. It does not follow that there is some sort of Reservoir of colour wash discreetly subsisting somewhere or other from which, on occasion, universals are drawn, to make bananas 'yellow', or acts of generosity 'good'.

Likewise with the soul. As is the case with universals, the words 'soul' or 'spirit' can (as we shall see) be given quite a respectable empirical placing. But we have to be very circumspect lest such words be made the topic of all kinds of misleading talk, with souls – and spirits – doing this, that and the other. Not that such talk – even about spirit huntsmen or spirit doctors – could not, in principle, be pegged back in a very complex fashion into one or a number of related disclosure-situations, and in that way be given a complicated justification. That may be. But we should need to exercise the highest degree of logical circumspection to make sure that any such developed doctrine of the soul or of spirits was not more misleading than useful.

Rather more positively, now, let us offer some considerations as to how, in general, useful talk about 'the soul' can be developed.

As a first move, perhaps it might be suggested that to avoid being misled by talk about the 'soul', it is useful to hold the doctrine of the resurrection of the body as a counterbalance. It would then be a case of two blacks making a white, for each phrase taken by itself is about as misleading as it could be. I need say no more than I have done in previous pages about the difficulties which can be generated by the phrase 'immortality of the soul'. As to the other phrase – 'resurrection of the body' – I am not suggesting that we think specifically of its use within Christian doctrine. For our present purpose it is useful and proper to recall that all kinds of religions have supposed the dead to appear again with, at any rate, bodies of some kind – hence we have the swords, drinking vessels, food and the like, which are found in ancient graves. Whereupon we face the difficulties: what then of the nitrogen cycle? What indeed of the facts covered by the Yorkshire folk song 'On Ilkla Moor baht hat' – a song which leaves us in no doubt as to our biological decomposition? And yet we have to admit that the doctrine of the resurrection of a body,[1] like the occurrence in graves of such objects as we have mentioned, at any rate has the merit of suggesting that 'immortality' is not thought of as a quality characterising some curious thing called a 'soul'. For a person's soul could not eat food or wear swords, though of course people have spoken of the soul having 'heavenly food', wearing an 'invisible sword' or a 'sword of the spirit' and so on. But that only shows how counterpart language is likely to develop, and though it may (as we have admitted) have some point to make, we have been more concerned to emphasise how likely it is to be misleading unless we make its particular logical structure clear. So, difficulties aside, the doctrine of the resurrection of the body and the doctrine of the immortality of the soul, if (despite, indeed as a result of, their inadequacy when taken singly) taken together to make complementary claims, might well be regarded as plotting from two opposite points of view what the phrase 'immortality of I' talks about. The one

---

[1] At this point I deliberately say 'a' and not 'the' to cover the doctrine in its most general version.

doctrine – the resurrection of the body – reminds us that to understand what 'my immortality' talks about, public behaviour stories will be relevant and necessary; the other doctrine – the immortality of the soul – reminds us that such stories will never themselves be adequate. For however the phrase 'the soul' is to be used, no one has ever, or would ever, claim that it relates to public behaviour and nothing more – though some (as we have seen) have come close to this,[1] and many have talked of it as if it were some 'thing' existing in some shadowy realm.

These remarks have, I suppose, despite their generality, inevitably reminded us of the Christian position, which in an endeavour to explicate and talk about 'eternal life',[2] has often used, albeit in a very uneasy relationship, both the doctrines we have just mentioned. In recent days, however, there have been various attempts by theologians, some to by-pass and others to condemn any doctrine of the immortality of the soul in an endeavour to stress what would be called a more Hebraic tradition. Now whatever we may think of these attempts (and we shall discuss the Christian position in a little more detail later)[3] it might perhaps be useful and interesting at this point to remind ourselves of the Hebraic approach. For this approach is at least notable in never having let itself talk of 'souls' in such a way as has been commonplace, for instance, amongst many later Christian philosophers, and which as we have seen lays itself open to much misunderstanding. What suggestion can the Old Testament offer us about the logical geography of the word 'soul'?

We might say that the Hebrews approached the subject of a man's existence in a way which fits well with the disclosure-situations we have been emphasising. While it is true that the Hebrews might, at the first, have regarded man as a 'unity' which was no more than the togetherness of his public behaviour (when they had no belief in his immortality), it is equally true

---

[1] See pp. 101ff.
[2] Or what is more aptly called 'eternal life in Christ Jesus'. See p. 144 below.   [3] See below, pp. 143ff.

that at a later date man was another sort of 'unity', that 'unity' which was this public behaviour *and more*. To express this later claim the Hebrews talked of his public behaviour being 'breathed into', we might say 'enlivened' or activated. So it happened as we have already noted[1] that the Hebrews began to think of a man as more than his public behaviour, as 'immortal', when, and only when, they began to conceive him as being deliberately responsible for his activity.

At this point, then, the 'unity' of a 'person' has been given in a disclosure-situation. 'Unity' had now become a metaphysical word, whereas before it described no more than a somewhat complex group of observable features. There was no question, however, at this second stage of thinking that a 'soul' had been added to a person's 'body'. The whole man had become a transcendent unity – an 'ensouled body' – a unity not limited to the external behaviour it exhibited. Incidentally, it is important to recognise if we are to do justice to the Hebraic position, that even at the first stage there is a place for *some* disclosure. The Hebrews were always a religious people. But at the first stage the disclosure was not around the individual, it occurred only at a group level. To give the background to this first stage quite briefly: the idea would be that we might talk of the public behaviour of this man and that man, and that man . . . and so on, until at a certain point a disclosure occurred. This would be the way in which to discover the empirical basis and justification for talking of a 'people chosen by God'. But our present concern is not with this background to earlier beliefs; it is rather to insist that at neither the earlier nor the later stage did the Hebrews suppose that the 'soul' was a logical counterpart of 'body'. This was a theme which Christian doctrine developed through a Greek-Latin-Scholastic tradition. Nor of course, as I have emphasised, can we say outright that for us to use the word 'soul' to stand for what transcends our public behaviour, is *wrong*. But we can certainly urge that the greatest care will then be needed about the way we develop this talk

[1] See p. 79 above.

about the soul, and on the whole we would judge that the language of the Hebrews is liable to be logically less misleading than language – whatever its origin, or development – where we are much more strongly tempted to think of the soul as a counterpart existent to a body. Let us take some examples, almost at random, of the way the Old Testament talks of 'souls':

(i) 'And the Lord formed man of the dust of the ground, and breathed into his nostrils the breath of life; and man became *a living soul*' (i.e. distinctively a 'person'). Gen. 2.7.

(ii) 'Then shall they give every man a ranson *for his soul* unto the Lord, when thou numberest them.' (Those who are numbered are individuals, 'men', not 'persons'. So it becomes imperative for the existence of something beyond a man's numerical unity to be acknowledged. Something must be done to do justice to 'his soul' = to 'himself' as a 'person'.) Ex. 30.12.

(iii) 'Thy friend, which is *as thine own soul*' (i.e. as thyself). Deut. 13.6.

(iv) 'Thou shalt love the Lord thy God with all thine heart, and *with all thy soul* (i.e. with all thy personality), and with all thy might.' Deut. 6.5.

(v) 'The soul of Jonathan was knit with the soul of David, and Jonathan loved him *as his own soul*' (i.e. as himself. The soul of Jonathan = all that public behaviour which was 'Jonathan' and more.) I Sam. 18.1; 20.17.

(vi) 'I also could speak as you do; If *your soul* were *in my soul's stead*, I could join words together against you' (your soul = your self; my soul = myself). Job 16.4.

(vii) '*My soul* is continually in my hand.' (= My life is continually exposed to constant peril.) Ps. 119.109.

We can see from these few examples that the word 'soul' was so used as to be a synonym for 'I' or 'person', where 'person' describes the whole living being – 'objects' and more. This is typical of the Hebraic approach[1] and there is perhaps an echo

[1] In fact *nephesh* is given for its dictionary translations the following words: 'breath, life; soul, mind; living being, creature, person, self.'

in the well-known comment expressive of deep feeling: 'He's a good soul', or in the international distress signal interpreted as 'Save our Souls'. Here is no invitation to some metaphysical salving operation, but rather a request to recognise circumstances in which ships' passengers have become 'persons', bearers of a transcendent moral claim, in response to which all action is to be subordinated. 'Save our souls' = 'Save us, as persons with more than passenger-unit significance.' It is such 'souls' which are immortal.

In short, my conclusion is that the philosopher can welcome the contemporary Christian emphasis on the Hebrew use of the word 'soul', which is a much better guide to its logical behaviour than language which suggests that the soul is some kind of counterpart, but hidden, object.[1] The Hebrews showed implicit logical good sense when, as we have already remarked in a footnote, they used the 'immortality of the soul' as a synonym for the 'immortality of I'.

So far, then, we have tried to show what logical behaviour must be given to phrases like 'immortality', 'eternal life' and 'timeless self' if they are to be unmistakably grounded in the kind of situation which we have earlier argued that it is the function of arguments for immortality to evoke. We have also tried to explicate the most satisfactory logical placing for the word 'soul'. It must not be talked of as if it were some sort of

---

[1] Cp. some remarks by Dr L. W. Grensted in 'The changing background of Theological Studies', *Bulletin of the John Rylands Library*, Vol. 37, No. 1, Sept. 1954, pp. 33, 36: 'The difference (between the Latin and Greek approaches) may be readily seen by noting that the familiar phrase *mens sana in corpore sano* cannot be translated directly into Greek at all. No Greek word for mind, such as νοῦς or διάνοια will fit the sentence. They are all too functional to carry the adjective. A man may be healthy in his thinking, but he has not a thing called a mind which can be healthy as a body is healthy. It is in such matters as these that the modern criticism of language may, I hope, renew and vitalize our study of the ways in which the terms of Greek philosophy became, in the fourth and fifth centuries, fitted to the usages of common Christian speech, with the legalists and administrators of the Latin West struggling to keep pace with their thought, failing again and again to appreciate its deeper reality of meaning, and thinking all the time that they were leading the way.'

occult counterpart to a body. 'Soul' works rather like the word 'I' or 'person', and if we are asked what is immortal, the best answer we can give is 'I'.

We shall now try, as we promised, to make some suggestions about the logical geography of a somewhat more complex area, viz. discourse about immortality in terms of a 'future life'.

V

LANGUAGE ABOUT IMMORTALITY: A 'FUTURE' LIFE

SOME PAGES AGO,[1] following on the suggestion that 'I' is the least misleading answer to be given to the question 'What is immortal?', we asked: is this, then, to have immortality without any talk of a future life? How, on this view, do we cash assertions about 'the life to come'? We promised at a later stage to face up to this kind of question by offering some suggestions about the kind of logical structure that can be given to various doctrines of a future life, when it is recognised that such doctrines will have to gain their empirical significance by being pegged back in the end into an 'immortality' situation. To this talk we now turn.

At the outset let us recognise that all doctrines of a future life, whatever their variety, are alike in one important respect. They all arise as so many versions of one answer to a general logical problem which everyone who formulates religious language must face. The problem is this. In acknowledging any religious topic whatever, we acknowledge something which exceeds the spatio-temporal. But how can we talk about what thus exceeds 'objects', when the only common public ground between us all is language about the spatio-temporal, language about those 'objects'? Where can we find language about 'objects' which might provide suitable currency for what is not spatio-temporally cut and dried, for what is not wholly restricted to 'objects' such as are seen, touched, and the rest?

[1] See p. 104.

The first move by way of an answer to this problem is to recognise that since the disclosure-situation is such that it cannot (logical *cannot*) be wholly restricted to 'objects', no story told about 'objects' can possibly be suitable currency for such a disclosure if it ever comes to an end. For if an 'object' story ever came to an end, if an 'object' story were ever finite, it would by that very fact lose its chance of talking about what is spatio-temporal *and more*. But where do we find infinite object-stories which are never-ending? One answer to this question, and for our present purpose the most important answer, is: in all talk about a 'future life'. All such talk about the future, being necessarily talk about a *never-ending* series of 'objects', about objects which go on for ever and ever . . . is likely therefore to be useful as currency for a situation which no number of 'objects' ever exhausts.[1] Here is the point of, and the broad justification for talking of immortality in terms of a 'future life'.

To make clearer the logical device which is being employed, an illustration from mathematics might perhaps be useful. If someone draws a series of circles centres O_1, O_2, O_3, $O_4 \ldots O_n$ respectively, and draws to each circle diameters $A_1 O_1 B_1$, $A_2 O_2 B_2 \ldots A_n O_n B_n$ respectively:

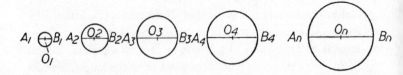

we might 'see' at once that the ratio of the circumference of any circle centre O_r to its diameter $A_r O_r B_r$ was constant. Such a conclusion might strike us by inspection; it would then occur in a disclosure-situation. If it did, we would know what is meant by the symbol π. In the same way (we have argued) it is by a disclosure-situation that we know what is meant by 'immortality'.

But suppose, now, we want some way of 'calculating' π, of

---

[1] Cp. the suggestion on p. 74 above.

talking about it to all and sundry, and whether or not they have the geometrical 'insight' demanded by the first exercise. We might then talk of π in relation to symbols 1, 2, 3 . . . used in other contexts. We can then prove that

$$\frac{\pi}{4} = 1 - \frac{1}{3} + \frac{1}{5} - \frac{1}{7} + \frac{1}{9} \ldots$$

But we have succeeded in getting this 'straightforward' account of π only at the cost of formulating an unending series of terms through all future time. Further, in such a series, extending indefinitely into the future, we would only be ever approximating to what, in one good sense of the word, we 'knew' all along; having known it when the first, geometrical, exercise succeeded, and the disclosure occurred.

So with talk of a 'future life'. 'Immortality' tells of something of which we can be aware here and now; the word belongs to a present disclosure. To believe we are immortal is to recognise now a certain sort of situation. But if we wish to explicate this situation, to talk of it to those who may not already recognise it, to use of it words which have an agreed use in other contexts – it is in terms of a story about an unending future that we shall do it.

Having seen then how stories of a future life can in principle be apt currency for the immortality situation, we next ask: how in particular may blueprints for such stories be constructed? To begin with, whence do we derive the concept of what in its most developed form is a time series unending in each direction – doubly-infinite serial time?

It is certainly important to remind ourselves at the outset that all language about a 'future life' which we might use in discourse about immortality must be regarded, from a logical point of view, as a highly intellectual construction. This remark I now propose to elucidate and justify.

No one has done more to clear our minds on this topic than A. N. Whitehead,[1] who suggests that to make clear the complex structure which such language possesses we must begin with

[1] See *The Concept of Nature*, Cambridge, 1919, Chs. III and IV.

what the psychologists call, albeit misleadingly, 'the specious present'. For if anything deserves to be called 'specious' it is the idea of the present as a 'moment of no duration', a concept which so many believe to be reliable and respectable. On the contrary, the 'present' is what is presented now; and what is here and now is something perfectly recognisable which includes a finite time-span. Further, it has what might be called 'temporal flow'. It is characterised by a direction: earlier to later. Thirdly, it contains overlapping events. Throughout the whole of some such specious present a siren may be sounding, and during part of the time a bell may be chiming so that the noise of the chime is superimposed on the continuous siren. Here is an example of 'overlapping': siren over bell. Or we may have a hydraulic drill giving a rhythmic pattern of noise throughout the whole of another specious present. Within this a whistle may be blown, and while the whistle is being blown a single note of a piano may be struck or the string of a violin plucked. In this way we can have another picture of overlapping events; drill over whistle; drill or whistle over a single note from the piano or violin. Whitehead's suggestion, expressed without the refinement of the complications he mentions,[1] would be that a 'moment' is a cluster of such overlapping events which might be pictured as each related to the other as one Chinese box to that which it next contains. A moment would be a class of such events which converge towards a particular point. A succession of such 'moments', ordered by the relation of temporal flow, gives us what we mean by an infinite serial time-order. Language about a future life starts from such a complex beginning as this: it is, in this way, a highly intellectual construction from the language we use about what is seen and heard.

Next let us notice that while we now have a reliable account of an infinite series of moments, we have no reason whatever to assume on that account that 'life' after death is to be regarded

---

[1] E.g. in his *Process and Reality*, Cambridge, 1929, Pt. IV, Ch. III, though the reader going there for more details is warned not to expect too easy reading.

as temporally *continuous* with this life. Our picture of a continuous temporal series which, as 'infinite' inevitably extends
beyond death, is only a rough way of working out the significance
of what is given to us *now* in our intimation of immortality. It
is no more than a first approximation. There is no reason to
suppose that after death there will be events in a time-series
continuous with the present one. In fact, since at death all our
public behaviour undergoes a characteristic and decisive change
it might well be claimed that all the evidence was in the other
direction. We might perhaps put the point like this: that if we
may speak of spatio-temporal events after death, we cannot
reasonably suppose they will do other than constitute a time-
series discontinuous with the present one, a series which cannot
easily, to say the least, be given a temporal relation to the time-
series we know at present.

The next suggestion, then, if we wish to talk of immortality
in terms of a future life, is that we should talk of it in terms of
discontinuous time-periods. Further, it may happen that by
speaking of such discontinuities the trans-temporal character
of an immortality situation is made more evident. For, just as
five discontinuous planes may specify what is 'supra-planar',
e.g. an open three-dimensional box, do we not naturally expect
that there is something 'supra-temporal' about whatever has to
be talked about in terms of several discontinuous time-periods?
Here is a philosophical approach to what has been called in
theological language an 'age' or an 'aeon'.[1] Here, too, is the
philosophical background to one of the earliest Christian accounts
of a disclosure-situation (where the author was 'in the Spirit'),[2]
which is given in terms of a 'future life'. In the Apocalypse we
are told of a 'new' ($\kappa\alpha\iota\nu\acute{o}s$) heaven and a 'new' earth, where the
first heaven and the first earth had 'passed away' ($=\dot{\alpha}\pi\hat{\eta}\lambda\theta\alpha\nu$).[3]

---

[1] Given a specially Christian interpretation in, e.g., A. Nygren,
Commentary on Romans, trans. C. C. Rasmussen, London, 1952, p. 24.
See also J. Marsh, *The Fulness of Time*, New York/London, 1952,
e.g. p. 31. [2] Rev. 1.10.
[3] Rev. 21.1: $\kappa\alpha\iota\nu\acute{o}s$ specifies the 'new' in contrast to the outworn,
the effete, whereas for example '$\nu\acute{e}os$' would be the most recent

Night and day – the primitive measures of time here and now – had disappeared – there was neither sun nor moon.[1] Here is discontinuity indeed.

But much language about a future life, overlooking the likelihood of several discontinuous time-periods, and reverting to our earlier suggestion, has preferred to work in terms of *one continuous* time-series, where life goes on and on for ever. Death is seen as 'but a gate' on a continuous road leading into endless life. Yet even passing over the difficulty we have already noted, there is a second and major difficulty in so handling a trans-temporal theme in terms of a continuous time-series. I am not thinking at the moment of the question as to whether 'future life' language in such a case needs supplementing by talk about an infinite 'past life' as well – that is a further question we must glance at later.[2]

The major difficulty arises in this way. If we talk of immortality in terms of a never-ending object story – a going on and on and on – there is always a risk that such language will be misread. It may be supposed in short that our immortality does not differ significantly from the survival of a stone, which merely goes on and on. For by itself, language talking about a never-ending series of objects will not necessarily make plain its trans-temporal reference. There is always the risk that in this way an object story which merely goes on and on and on will conceal rather than reveal the point for which it is being used. It will therefore hardly serve by itself and in an unmodified form as reliable currency for a disclosure such as an immortality-situation undoubtedly is. As I have said, to talk of immortality in terms of a continuous never-ending life may altogether fail to reveal the trans-temporal character of an immortality-situation. The 'future life' may seem no more than an unending journey within a single time-period. Cp. R. C. Trench, *Synonyms of the New Testament*, § lx, where he concludes his discussion: '*Νέος* ad tempus, *καινός* ad rem refertur.' For 'passed away' implying disappearance and the substitution of a new discontinuous order, cp. Enoch 91.16, 'the first heaven will depart and pass away, and a new heaven will appear'. Here are claims for discontinuity.

[1] Rev. 21.23.   [2] See pp. 136ff.

where we reach every station only to discover that there is at least one more to come; or some unending feast where whatever course we reach, we discover there is at least one more to follow. And there need be nothing religious about either activity.

Therefore in one way or another any story of a continuous future life will have to be complicated and developed, so as to make it clear beyond doubt and from the start, that these serial stories have a 'more-than-objects' point to make.

By way of illustration and without claiming to be exhaustive in our account of the logical geography of a future life, we shall give examples of two kinds of such developed stories. The first kind, (*a*), endeavours by a supplementary claim to bring out beyond any oversight or misunderstanding the full significance of the infinite, unending character of the story. The second kind, (*b*), in constructing its language about the future, uses stories which are specially likely and already apt to evoke disclosure-situations. In this way it offers us an alternative possibility for ensuring that no one overlooks the 'more than objects' claim of language about a future life, when such language is offered as currency for an immortality-situation.

(*a*) The first type of story which talks in terms of a continuous future, avoids the risk of seeming to talk of our immortality as though it were the 'immortality' or survival of a brick, by insisting that to its story of a future life, there shall be necessarily attached the concept of an 'End'. The future life has some critical occasion associated with it: it is no *mere* going on, and on and on . . . just like that. It is in this way, by specifying some critical limit, that such language about a future life attempts to be reliable and adequate currency for an immortality-situation; it attempts to make clear beyond misunderstanding its grounding in a disclosure. So arises talk about the 'End' of history, or about the 'end' of time. Here is a 'Day of the Lord', a 'Golden Age' seen as a 'goal of history'; here is 'the end' when history is fulfilled and completed with God as 'all in all'.[1] In theological

---

[1] These two examples, taken almost at random, happen to come from H. H. Rowley's *The Rediscovery of the Old Testament*, London,

doctrines such as these, there is presupposed, I am suggesting, a never-ending story about the future, whose success in telling a trans-temporal tale is consequently ensured by having associated with it the concept of an 'End', an 'End' which cannot, without involving a flat contradiction, be a mere term in the never-ending series, to which it is nevertheless related. In this way the reference of talk about immortality to something beyond an endless series of observables is made plain.

Now have we outside theology any parallel to this use of language which, while talking of what goes on and on and on, nevertheless talks also of an 'End'? Are we able to find anywhere outside theology a clue to the logic of 'End' as this type of story uses it?

At this point we may pause for a moment to reflect that some would say that these questions are misplaced; that theology is *sui generis*; that patterns of arguments occurring elsewhere can have no parallel in theological discussion.[1] All the same I venture to draw what I believe is an important parallel, suggesting once again that the paradoxical language of mathematics may illuminate the paradoxical language of theology, that the mathematician and the theologian may find some kind of logical meeting-place.

My suggestion here is that the use of 'End' in theological language about 'immortality' is reminiscent of the use of 'limit' in mathematical language about (say) a function of a positive integral variable. For example, the sequence $\frac{1}{2}$, $\frac{2}{3}$, $\frac{3}{4}$, $\frac{4}{5}$ ... approaches ever closer to, it tends to, the limit 1; 1 is a concept which somehow expresses the character of the sequence, and we might even call it the 'end' of the sequence. But the never-ending

1946, (title and theme of Ch. XI) and from I Cor. 15.24 respectively. It should of course be remembered though that there are other doctrines about an 'end' which do not conform to this logical pattern. As Dr John Marsh points out in *The Fulness of Time*, p. 126, the concept of 'the end' is used in many strands 'well-nigh inextricably confused', and here I only claim that there are *some* doctrines of 'the end' which illustrate my present point. The logical mapping of the many divers strands awaits someone's attention.

[1] Cp. Alasdair MacIntyre, *Metaphysical Beliefs*, London, 1957, p. 211 where he remarks that belief cannot argue with unbelief.

sequence never reaches it; it never includes 1 as one of its terms. Some readers may not be at all helped by the development of this example; and they may wish to pass immediately to page 126. Others may think the example is worth developing in rather more detail, and wish to see how close the mathematical parallel can be pressed. It is for them that these next pages are included.

Simplifying the matter somewhat for our present purposes, let us consider what happens to a function of n, (say) $\dfrac{n}{n+1}$, as n assumes successively the values 1, 2, 3. . . . As G. H. Hardy expressed it in his classical introduction[1]:

> The word 'successively' naturally suggests succession in time, and we may suppose n, if we like, to assume these values at successive moments of time (e.g. at the beginnings of successive seconds). Then as the seconds pass, n gets larger and larger and there is no limit to the extent of its increase. However large a number we may think of (e.g. 2,147,483,647), a time will come when n has become larger than this number.

In short, the successive evaluation of $\dfrac{n}{n+1}$ for $n = 1, 2, 3 \ldots$ can be usefully taken to represent the various terms of a future story, developing through successive 'moments' – 'the beginnings of successive seconds' – without end. We obtain, for instance, as n increases from 1 through the various integers, the following successive terms:

$$\tfrac{1}{2}, \tfrac{2}{3}, \tfrac{3}{4}, \tfrac{4}{5}, \tfrac{5}{6}, \tfrac{6}{7}, \tfrac{7}{8} \ldots \tfrac{100}{101}, \tfrac{101}{102} \ldots \text{ and so on.}$$

On surveying this sequence the reader may perhaps 'see' that these terms are approaching nearer and nearer to 1. We say, roughly speaking, that $\dfrac{n}{n+1}$ tends to the *limit* 1 when $\dfrac{n}{n+1}$ becomes nearly equal to 1 as n continues to increase. Rather more precisely, we say that $\dfrac{n}{n+1}$ tends to the limit 1 when no

---

[1] G. H. Hardy, *A Course of Pure Mathematics*, Cambridge, 1908, Ch. IV, § 55, p. 112.

matter how small a number (say, δ) is selected, there will be some value for n – say n_0 – such that the difference between $\frac{n_0}{n_0+1}$ and 1 will be smaller than δ for all values of n greater than or equal to n_0. Here then is one case of an unending sequence of terms tending nevertheless to a limit, and being in this way associated with some quite specific number.

For our purpose, there are three important points to notice in the illustration:

(i) Although in a popular kind of way we might picture the limit very roughly as the 'last term' of the sequence, it is plain on reflection that there is no such 'last term', and that the limit – in this case 1 – is never reached as the value of any term.

(ii) Nevertheless the limit arises out of the sequence and represents its character. It expresses something that we may say is anticipated by every term, and all sequences of terms. In an important way it typifies the sequence. For some sequences tend to no limits, e.g. the sequence represented by n or $\frac{n+1}{2}$. Such sequences just grow and grow as n increases. But the sequence represented in $\frac{n}{n+1}$ is distinctively different.

(iii) The limit will as a matter of fact be given in a moment of disclosure when we 'see' that number to which the sequence tends. For though we may write $\frac{n}{n+1}$ as $\left(1-\frac{n}{n+1}\right)$ we can never, mechanical-like, insert any value for n so that $\frac{1}{n+1}=0$.

We just have to 'see' that, as n continues to increase, $\frac{1}{n+1}$ approaches 0 more nearly that we could ever have cared to mention, so that since $\frac{n}{n+1}$ can be expressed as $\left(1-\frac{1}{n+1}\right)$ we are left with the limit of our sequence as 1.

Each of these points has an echo in the theological case. First, though we may picture the 'End' or the 'Last Things' very roughly as though it were a 'last term' of a very long sequence, it is plain that such a popular conception cannot for long be justified. There can be no straight 'end' to a never-ending series. We certainly cannot date the 'End' as we might attempt to date the next election. To date the 'End' is a logical impossibility. A date for the 'End' could neither be true nor false; it would be no more than mere brawling, and would show how confused we were about the logic of the language we were using. We can be quite unmoved by those who would predict the 'end of the world' in (say) 1978. But it is not only the unorthodox who have made logical blunders. Consider by way of illustration the following paragraph from Dr J. A. T. Robinson's *Jesus and his Coming*.[1]

> But the mistake lay not in the very conception of a future *Parousia*, which, despite occasional crudities, represents in dramatic terms a vivid and profound picture of the summing up of all things in Christ. What went wrong was when this picture, this myth, was taken for a literal event, a second event parallel with the first, lying on the same temporal line, and separated from it by an interval, whose length could be measured, 'if not now, then immediately after the second has happened'.*

* Minear, *The Christian Hope and the Second Coming*, p. 75.

In short, the logic of *Parousia*, in its late[2] significance of 'Second Coming', is the logic of 'The End' as we have understood it, and 'what went wrong' (or at least part of what went wrong) was when this was thought to describe 'a second event', a term of the series.

All the same, and secondly, the concept of 'End' or 'Last Things' can be, and must be, closely associated with the infinite sequence of future terms. Such phrases, indeed, mark its character. They show that what is important about the sequence is not that it goes on and on and on, but that it is meant to picture a disclosure, in relation to which (and here is the third

[1] London, 1957, pp. 180-1.   [2] For original use, see p. 124.

parallel) phrases like 'The End' or 'Last Things' – as well as the serial language associated with them, are alone properly understood.

So an 'End' or 'Last things' can be as reasonably associated with a never-ending story about the future, as a 'limit' can be associated with a never-ending sequence. In the latter case, to talk of a 'limit' implies that the particular sequence has a special character which is recognized in a 'disclosure'. In the former case 'End' and 'Last things' witness to the fact that the sequence to which they refer is not dissimilarly related to a disclosure-situation.

What these reflections amount to in the Christian case (which can again be taken by way of an illustrative example) is this: The Christian appeals to a specific disclosure situation which, with our present interest, we might call the *Parousia* in the sense in which that word was *originally* used in the New Testament. But to expound and to *talk about* this Parousia in an extended theology demands language (i) about the work and ministry of Jesus of Nazareth, (ii) about the continuing of this work, whether this be interpreted in terms of the Paraclete (the Fourth Gospel) or the Church (St Paul). But there must also be, besides this language capable of spanning an infinite extension of time, language (iii) about an 'End', if the character of the original *Parousia* is to be unambiguously presented and exposed.[1]

[1] See Dr. J. A. T. Robinson, *loc. cit.* It will be clear that I value greatly Dr Robinson's account of the changes in New Testament language about eschatology. Further, as I have said, I agree that 'the other half of Christian eschatology' (i.e. what is other than the finished work of Jesus) 'is not an event at all' (p. 183). I agree that it is not 'another event, at a measurable interval from the first, for which Christians must now, and always, be skinning their eyes' (p. 183). But I have tried to argue that, admitting these points, it will still be the case that we must have two languages admittedly differing in logic to *talk about* that *Parousia* (in the original sense) which is the label for that distinctively Christian disclosure which as such cannot but be complete and final, though our understanding of it and our language about it may never be likewise final and complete. So I would wish to allow for an element in Christian theology about 'the End' which some might think that Dr Robinson comes near to denying altogether when, and rightly, he condemns errors and blunders which have arisen from its misunderstanding and misallocation.

In this way *if its logical variegation is recognised*, Christian doctrine provides us with an apt illustration of how language can be used according to our first alternative to talk of what is known in a disclosure situation – be it called *Parousia* or *Eternal Life*.

We may express the point like this:

(i) 'The End' does *not* describe an event occurring at some point or other within that never-ending succession of 'moments' in terms of which we construct, and represent to ourselves the future.

(ii) This has been recognised by those, for example, who have spoken of 'the End' as a 'myth'; and they were plainly right in so far as such a classification was an attempt to give expression to the negative point that the logical behaviour of 'the end' is other than that of a phrase describing some event in time. But to call it – positively – a myth, has its dangers and is more than likely to be misunderstood. For it seems to make theology a fairy story, to set eschatology – the doctrine of the Last Things – alongside the 'myths' of Scandinavia or Greece.

(iii) What I have suggested is a way of avoiding this unfortunate positive conclusion to which we may misleadingly be brought. My point is that 'the End' is a phrase to be taken along with, and essentially connected with, the never-ending serial story, the whole range of this language – no matter how logically complex – being then seen as absolutely unavoidable if we are, on this first alternative, to talk satisfactorily about a disclosure situation which is 'observables' and more. The justification 'in fact' for stories about 'the End' is not a fairyland or Valhalla or Olympus, but that disclosure-situation which exceeds any number, however many, of spatio-temporal 'observables'.

A doctrine of the 'Last Things', then, far from compromising theology, is, on this first alternative for language about immortality, a *sine qua non* if such language is ever to make clear its distinctively religious – 'observables and more than observables' – claim.

So we conclude our discussion of this first alternative for language about immortality, language which while it talks of a never-ending sequence of terms talks also of an 'End' or 'Last Things'. We have seen (I hope) that such talk about an immortality situation can be defended, but only when the phrase 'the End' or 'Last Things' is given a logical status very similar to that of a mathematical 'limit'. Language about immortality, on this first alternative, can be paralleled with mathematical talk about an infinite sequence which is bounded, and then becomes appropriate currency for that immortality-situation which exceeds the spatio-temporal elements it contains. Otherwise, if our talk is not of an endless future which is (so to say) 'bounded', our language is not likely to provide currency suited to a disclosure-situation such as we are appealing to in our justification of immortality. In such a case we are not likely to be able to distinguish between the survival of a stone – a mere going on and on and on – and our immortality.

(*b*) This brings us to our second brand of language about immortality which in yet another way tries to ensure that serial language about the future is suitable currency for an immortality-situation. On this alternative, language about a future life incorporates, as basic units, phrases whose grounding in disclosure-situations is already recognised and admitted. In this way we seek to guarantee its transcendent reference from the start. Otherwise, as currency for immortality, stories of a future life whose basic theme is feasting, or sheer inactivity, start with an enormous liability. It is just about as hard to make an endless feast currency for a disclosure-situation, as to make a plate of sausages an occasion for worship. Better to use as units in our future life-story, phrases which already have likely disclosure-possibilities.

We may take three examples. The first takes stories of characteristically personal behaviour which are associated with purposiveness, and sets these as units in the story of a future life.

(i) For instance, we might see on a beach some stones formed into a circular arc. But there might be nothing specially striking about such a formation. We might talk about it in terms of the tide, the currents, the slope of the beach, and so on. But suppose now that on the beach we see a figure of eight, or perhaps someone's name, made up from pebbles, and that all round these pebbles the beach shows only clean sand. Here would be a pattern likely to evoke a disclosure-situation. We should talk of the pattern being indicative of purposiveness, of deliberate personal activity, and so on, where such phrases, as we saw in Chapters I and II, are indicative of a situation such as that which justifies talk about immortality. Hence it becomes possible to talk of our immortality in terms of purpose patterns which are in some sort of way continuous through and beyond death. In this way a believer in immortality expresses his belief by talking, like Butler, of his whole life on earth as a 'state of probation', i.e. as a pattern continuous with a pattern beyond death, and the whole forming one purpose. In this way, a belief in immortality expresses itself by talking of a purposiveness which finds its fulfilment beyond this life.

It will, I think, be instructive to take as an illustration of this kind of language about immortality, a discussion which can be found in O. C. Quick's *Doctrines of the Creed*[1] not least because it enables us at the same time to link our present reflections with those we have already made on language about 'the End' and 'Last Things'. Dr Quick:

(A) argues that the 'notion of something which happens strictly last in time' is contradictory, and

(B) suggests that the word 'last' or 'final' should rather be taken to refer 'not simply to that which comes after everything else, but to that which completes a process by bringing it to its purposed end'. He says later: 'When the word "last" is used in relation to purpose, "the last thing" does not denote simply or mainly the thing which comes after all others in a series, but that which fulfils the purpose of the whole.' In this way, to use Dr Quick's own examples, the artist, in his work of art, comes to the last stroke of his brush, and the traveller to Edinburgh

---

[1] London, 1938, Pt. III, Ch. XXII. See pp. 245-8. What is essentially the same kind of discussion will also be found in A. E. Taylor, *Does God Exist?*, London, 1945, pp. 71-73.

sets foot in the end on Waverley Station. But the picture and the journey, says Dr Quick, find their significance in what now follows as the 'fulfilment' of the particular purpose, which of course includes the actual work of painting or travelling respectively. So he would suggest that 'last things' rather relates to the fulfilment of a purpose and 'derives its special importance from what is *beyond* the series of events of which it is the last'. As he has said earlier, 'A mere last event' (for example, the last stroke of the artist's brush) 'does not at all derive its special importance from the fact that it happens to come after all the others, but from the fact that it completes the whole', and (we may presumably say) makes us the better prepared for what follows. 'Last Things' are thus seen by Dr Quick as purpose-dividers, separating one purposive scheme from another. We may integrate Dr Quick's discussion with our own by making four points:

1. Dr Quick is rightly nervous about using 'Last Things' as descriptive. As we have seen earlier 'Last Things' in religious discourse does not work like the phrase might work in auctioneering discourse – to describe things that are reached when all else has been disposed of, a sort of ' Miscellaneous Lot (mainly Judgments)'.

2. Further, Dr Quick is right in so far as he implies that 'Last Things' must somehow or another be related to a 'whole', to a disclosure, to what 'strikes us' as we contemplate several units falling to a 'purposive whole'. For here (as we have just pointed out in this section) is something akin to an immortality-situation.

3. But this reflection shows that what in fact Dr Quick gives us in his suggestion is a way of talking not so much about the Last Things, as about an immortality-situation in terms of a succession of purposes – the kind of language we are designating as (*b*)(i). Dr Quick, I suggest, has rightly seen the kind of situation in which language about immortality must be founded; he has seen further that the phrase 'Last Things' is logically problematical, and what he has in fact consequentially done is to avoid the logical difficulty by moving to a very different logical

frame (in our classification from (*a*) to (*b*)(i)) – by moving to language about a continuous[1] future life whose unit is purposive stories.

4. But while this move saves him any logical embarrassment over 'Last Things', it is only done at a cost – the cost of shedding but little light on the characteristic use of that phrase, which is now no more than 'purpose divider'. 'Last Things' has lost any suggestion of 'unique finality'. We may put the point otherwise by saying that if Dr Quick alternatively claimed that his illustrations did something to help us *unite* languages (*a*) and (*b*)(i), and in this way had a welcome power of logical integration, it would be right to remark that the integration only gained at the expense of giving only a faint light on the characteristic logical behaviour of 'Last Things'. So, even considered as an attempt to illuminate the whole variegated complex of theological language about immortality, what is gained one way is lost another.

What we have suggested above is another model altogether – a mathematical one – by which to illuminate the logical behaviour of the phrase 'Last Things'. Thereafter we have now distinguished very firmly between language about immortality which talks respectively of 'Last Things' and of a continuous succession of purposes, though it is true that despite their logical differences both are similar in so far as by contrast with language portraying discontinuity[2] they presuppose language about a continuous never-ending future. So we come to our next example of language about a continuous future which uses, as units, stories of disclosure situations.

(ii) For the second example of language about the future which continues to talk of immortality by centring on disclosure-models, we may take the case where these models are moral stories, and in particular stories of rewards and punishments.

---

[1] It is true that Dr Quick speaks at one point of the 'notion of an unending series of events in time' being 'equally unthinkable', but I am not clear how in the end he links this – if he does – with his main suggestion to which for our present purpose I have confined our discussion.　　　　　　　　　　　　　　　　[2] See p. 117 above.

When we 'see' that such and such an activity 'deserves' this reward, or that punishment, a disclosure-situation (it would be claimed) has occurred. That at any rate is the presupposition of any use of language about rewards and punishments as a means of talking about a future life – language which has given rise to the traditional pictures of a Grand Assize and a Day of Reckoning.

We may here recall Butler's discussion in his *Analogy of Religion, Natural and Revealed, to the constitution and course of Nature*.[1] There he is specially concerned to defend the reasonableness of this kind of language for talk about a future life. 'Conscience', said Butler in effect, 'is definitive for life.' By it we recognise, in particular, that wrong-doing deserves punishment, and good behaviour deserves reward. Nor, he argued, have we any reason to suppose that all this will somehow, at death, be *utterly* changed beyond all recognition. It may or may not be, but we have no reason positively to suppose so, and (he said) we have, at the same time, some reason to assume a thread of continuity between our present life and a 'life beyond death'. So let us take over and extrapolate the language of future punishments and future rewards as a possible and apt way of talking about immortality.

Now it may be that today we have all kinds of misgivings about such language; the language of retribution is often, and at best, associated with no more than an impersonal justice, and consequently has no foundation in any disclosure situation. At one time it was altogether different. About two hundred years ago Kant could claim that 'Juridical punishment . . . must in all cases be imposed only because the individual on whom it is inflicted *has committed a crime*. . . . The penal law is a Categorical Imperative.'[2] Undoubtedly, for Kant, retribution expressed a quasi-religious 'demand' to be actualised, for this reason it was a 'categorical imperative' – all of which meant that

[1] See esp. Pt. I, Ch. III.
[2] Quoted from Kant's *Philosophy of Law* (E.T. by Hastie, 1887, p. 195) by H. Rashdall, *The Theory of Good and Evil*, Oxford, 1907, Vol. I, Ch. IX, p. 285 (italics original).

(for him) retribution was grounded in a disclosure-situation.

But nowadays people speak of retribution as an 'inveterate instinct of primitive humanity' which ought to have 'but little influence over our ideas of *human* justice'.[1] Retributive punishment is thought by many to be inhuman, indeed sub-human. The merely efficient warder and the merely efficient hangman no more belong to a disclosure-situation than the merely efficient doctor or the merely efficient butcher.[2]

As currency for immortality, therefore, the language of retribution is nowadays more likely to mislead than to be helpful, for it embodies nothing beyond what is spatio-temporally verifiable – a possibility which Joseph Butler in his day did not contemplate. For Butler, as for Kant, every judgment about retribution was grounded in a 'disclosure'. But whatever be our hesitation over the particular way in which he worked out his thesis, let us at any rate give Joseph Butler the credit for emphasising by his general discussion that the roots of immortality are to be found in the moral discernments of the present, and that language at once about morality and the future can in principle be good currency in terms of which to talk about immortality.

(iii) So to our third and last example. Of all the ways of talking about immortality perhaps the best, and certainly one which is far less likely than any other to lead into difficulties, is that which embodies in its language about the future, reference to characteristically personal situations. Of these situations, those most apt are such as can be described in terms of 'love' or, what the Christian would call *agape*. That this exceeds any and all public behaviour is evident from the context of I Corinthians 13. For there, we are told, *agape never* faileth, and beareth, hopeth and endureth *all things*. In short, we only know *agape* when it breaks in on us at some point or another as an endurance story is developed *without end*. We only know *agape* in a disclosure-situation exceeding the observables it contains. For

[1] *Loc cit.*, pp. 284, 285 (italics original).
[2] See pp. 29 and 65 respectively.

agape is nothing which any particular kind of public behaviour guarantees. 'Though I bestow all my goods to feed the poor' and show all kinds of social generosity; even 'though I give my body to be burned' – though I am quite consumed with working for such and such good causes – though I display all this admirable public behaviour, it may still be that I have missed *agape*. To possess this *agape* or love, is to possess that whose working out cannot be adequately talked of in 'object' stories. It is with this background that *agape*, or love, becomes ideal currency for immortality.

There is also a further appropriateness and advantage in talking of immortality in terms of personal affection or devotion. A friendship may be, and very often is, started by a quite distinctive act of self-giving, some total response to what is discerned in a 'moment of vision', a responsive act of loyalty which is all-embracing: what is on some occasions called 'falling in love'. Thereafter, as each person through the years develops his own possibilities, the friendship (we say) becomes through all vicissitudes mutually enriching. But in one good sense, the devotion and the friendship is never stronger or weaker than it was at the start. In one sense the 'bond' is the same from start to finish. It might be said indeed that life, as its years go by, only unravels and exposes all that the first act of loyalty embraced. At any rate, it is on this analogy that we can construct the least misleading serial pictures extending into the future of that which we can know already as our immortality.

Here is a clue to the logic of such language about immortality as is used, for example, in a popular hymn:

> Happy are they, they that love God
>   Whose hearts have Christ confest. . . .

> Sad were our lot, evil this earth,
>   Did not its sorrows prove
> The path whereby the sheep may find
>   The fold of Jesu's love.

Then shall they know, they that love him
How all their pain is good
And death itself cannot unbind
Their happy brotherhood.[1]

Here is the language of human love and friendship extended from the present through all vicissitudes and beyond death, and being thus used as currency for talking of 'immortality'.

So I conclude this section by suggesting that if language about a continuous future is to be developed as language about immortality according to this second method, it will at its best incorporate the theme of personal affection and devotion. With the language of rewards and punishments, and even with the language of purposiveness, we may well fail to see the precise way in which such language is being used to develop currency for immortality. We may fail to feed the language back into the disclosure-situation which alone justifies it. We should then have theological language without religion; talk of a future life but no immortality. At the same time, we must not forget our first alternative – the possibility of having language for immortality which ensured its disclosure reference by talk of an End[2]: which means that besides singing such a hymn as that quoted above, by C. Coffin, we shall be wise if we further include in our logical repertory at least such language as that provided, for example by the following hymn[3]:

---

[1] *The English Hymnal*, 398 (C. Coffin, Tr. Yattenden Hymnal).

[2] There is also of course the language of discontinuity which I exemplified from the Apocalypse (p. 117 above). If now we were to look for this theme in ordinary religious discourse such as a hymn, we might possibly exemplify it by reference to:

There's a Friend for little children
Above the bright blue sky. . . .
(*The English Hymnal*, 607, A. Midlane)

for the main theme of the hymn is 'otherness' and contrast: the Friend is unlike all 'our earthly friends', and what is vitally important about the 'crown', the 'song', the 'robe' and so on is that they are made as discontinuous as may be with our present existence being all very decidedly 'Above the bright blue sky'. This is the setting – six times repeated – for every other assertion in the hymn.

[3] *The English Hymnal*, 503 (B. S. Ingemann, Tr. S. Baring-Gould).

Through the night of doubt and sorrow
Onward goes the pilgrim band. . . .

One the object of our journey . . .

One the gladness of rejoicing
On the far eternal shore
Where the One Almighty Father
Reigns in love for evermore.

Here is immortality as a pilgrimage, a continuous progression, a life going on and on and on. . . . But logically this is inadequate. Hence the last, and succeeding, verse – however inelegant and abrupt from a literary point of view, however much it looks to be an afterthought – is from a logical standpoint absolutely essential:

Soon shall come the great awaking,
Soon the rending of the tomb;
Then the scattering of all shadows,
And the end of toil and gloom.

Its very abruptness and discontinuity in relation to previous verses is a measure of the change of logical key; and it is significant that not only is its theme 'the End', but that it displays rather characteristically the 'more than observables' point which (as we have suggested) is what talk about 'the End' is meant to ensure. Here is what remains when 'all shadows' have scattered, something which abides any and all spatio-temporal cataclysms – 'the rending of the tomb' is no observable cracking due to faulty concrete or second-quality marble.

This extended discussion has, I hope, given us an outline introduction to the logical complexity of theological language about immortality. We have in effect suggested three types of language by comparison with which such discourse can be illuminated; three types of language which we can bring alongside discourse about immortality to help us better to understand its characteristic moves and claims.

(I) By the first type our immortality is portrayed not so much as a continuous survival as an existence through various discontinuous time-periods. Further, we claimed that it is the possibility of talking about discontinuous time-periods which can bring out and emphasize the trans-temporal character of the immortality-situation. Be that as it may, the other two types of language have their own special ways of representing this trans-temporal character.

(II) The other two types of language ((a) and (b)) talk unashamedly about a continuous future. But they are subsequently complicated: (a) in the one case by talking also of an 'End' and (b) in the other case, by using as a basic unit for the final language (i) language about purposiveness, or (ii) language about moral retribution, or (iii) language about personal affection.

We might perhaps notice here how some of the concrete imaginative pictures associated with doctrines of immortality need for their full understanding two or more of these logically distinguishable languages. For example, the picture of a Grand Assize can be seen as an attempt to combine (a) and (b)(ii), language talking of an 'End' and future retribution; the doctrine of Purgatory might be seen as combining I and (b)(i) and (ii), language talking of discontinuous realms, purposiveness and future retribution, and so on. Again we might well interpret any 'great gulf'[1] between heaven and hell in terms of the spatio-temporal discontinuities talked of by (I), though I suppose that the possibility of some communication between the 'regions' presumably presupposes some further continuity.

But whatever might be said about the particular logical structures which can be discerned in the various imaginative pictures which have been associated with doctrines of immortality, what I have tried to show is how all the three types of language which we have distinguished in this section (I, II (a) and (b)) are in their different ways permissible and justifiable, as each illustrating a possible solution to the general problem of how to talk of immortality in terms of public language which

[1] Luke 16.26.

must then be so structured as to make the necessary appeal to, and be associated with, a present disclosure-situation which is 'objects' and more. It is therefore by having such types of language at hand that we should expect to be able most reliably to understand the structure, and to assess the quality, of discourse about immortality.

We shall now conclude this chapter with a few brief reflections on three themes closely related to the topic of immortality:

A. Pre-existence
B. Universalism
C. Distinctively Christian claims

A. *Pre-existence*

We may conveniently begin our discussion here by taking up a point we deliberately set aside a little while ago.[1] What have we to say about the possibility of constructing language about immortality by talking not of a never-ending series of *future* terms, but of a never-ending series of *past* terms?

Let us notice that however strange the question may seem, it only introduces us in fact to a new approach to the old doctrine of pre-existence. Further, points we have already made about future stories can be equally well made about any possible translation of immortality-belief into stories about the past.

Start by recalling stories whose theme is 'I have been here before', though no memories and no records of the narrator's life can be discovered to substantiate such a declaration. Quite unexpectedly a street of a landscape seems (we are told) 'strangely familiar'. Or again, there are the stories of animals which have a specially 'knowing look'. We imagine the possibility that one day this cat will speak, when we would discover who in fact is on the other side of those whiskers; perhaps some twelfth-century baron, or sixteenth-century merchant adventurer. All such stories are endeavours to talk of an immortality-situation in terms of a series of events leading backwards into

[1] See p. 118 above.

the past. Immortality is being talked of in terms of this world in earlier times, in terms of a past life, rather than a future life.

But at this point let us remind ourselves of what we said about discontinuity in relation to stories about the future. There we saw how any reference to 'before' or 'after', 'earlier' or 'later', was extremely problematical. Our earlier discussion thus suggests that pre-existence is best pictured not so much in terms of a continuous series of past events, as in terms of various discontinuous time-series. Now at this point we might usefully supplement that suggestion with one made by Mr J. W. Dunne. We might regard Dunne's view as taking yet further this idea of discontinuous time-series, and saying in effect that rather than suppose that the discontinuous time-series were nevertheless in some kind of higher-order temporal succession, why not suppose that these various time-series characterise our existence already at every point? So that, instead of speaking of a life 'before', or for that matter 'after' the present, we might rather talk of 'life' in realms or regions other than that realm or region in which most of our 'life' normally occurs; though any awareness of our existence in such realms may only be minimal and only granted to a few people on rare occasions, as, for example, in certain dreams. Still, as 'one person' we unite these realms, and if there is this link, it is not surprising (if the general picture holds) that we sometimes (e.g. in certain dreams) have a glimpse into our serial existence. But whatever we have to say about this developed picture, or Mr Dunne's fascinating treatment of it,[1] the special interest from our point of view is that it provides an alternative way of developing the theme of discontinuity, whether in relation to the 'past' or the 'future'. In this way we see that we might talk about our immortality in language very different either from the traditional stories of pre-existence or the traditional stories of a future life. There arises the possibility of yet another sort of language which may not only illuminate,

---

[1] See: *An Experiment with Time*, London, 1929 (in Faber paper covered Editions, 1958); *The Serial Universe*, London, 1934; *The New Immortality*, London, 1938.

but even perhaps provide us with a new contribution to, discourse about immortality.

At the same time it is useful here to alert ourselves to one or other of the logical moves which we have already found were necessary to safeguard the language about immortality when this language was about the future. In other words, we shall need to guard against the parallel difficulty in the case of pre-existence, to thinking of immortality as the persistent survival of the stone. To avoid the possibility of talking of immortality in terms of the persistent survival of many strata, we must do something to signify the partial character of any one or any number of these serial stories.

To do this we might claim, and this is close to Dunne's position, that an *infinite*, i.e. a never-ending number of these serial stories will be required for adequate discourse about immortality. In this case, the word 'person' comes naturally to have a logical status which is from the point of view of public, 'object', language appropriately odd. For having then to 'include' a *never-ending* number of serial terms, having then to refer to all public behaviour (present and prospective) in all realms *no matter how many*, 'person' takes on a logical behaviour not at all unlike that of the phrase 'infinite sum'. For its use is now given by reference to the disclosures which (we hope) will occur as this unending number of serial groups is successively surveyed: a disclosure which then includes all possible spatio-temporal terms and more. Here, then, in talk of an infinite number of serial existences is apt language for immortality. 'Person' understood in terms of 'infinite behaviour possibilities' is certainly 'immortal'.

Alternatively we might decide to be content with such serial stories as we have any empirical evidence of, and then, to avoid the 'persistent strata' difficulty, we might introduce (say) some sort of limit word uniting them all at the 'start'. Such a word would have a logical behaviour closely similar to that of the word 'End' we have discussed earlier.[1] Such a word, which

[1] See p. 119 above.

would be in this way a logical kinsman of 'End', would be 'Creation'. We might incidentally also wish to have such a word as 'End' providing for the 'unity' of the strata at the 'finish'. In any case little by little we become aware of the logical complexities of theological talking.

Meanwhile, it is interesting to recall that on the whole talk about a future life has been much more popular than talk of pre-existence. People have been perhaps all too ready to speak as if their existence began with (say) the first act of breathing, the first cry, and so on. But we must firmly emphasize that it is no more reasonable to take such public behaviour as an account of our beginning, than to take similar public behaviour – the last breath – as a satisfactory account of our end. So we may agree with McTaggart that the 'attitude of most western thinkers to the doctrine of pre-existence is curious'. He continues: 'Of the many who regard our life after the death of our bodies as certain or probable, scarcely one regards our life before the birth of those bodies as a possibility which deserves discussion.[1] And yet it was taught by Buddha and by Plato, and it is usually associated with the belief in immortality in the far east. Why should men who are so anxious today to prove that we shall live after this life is ended, regard the hypothesis that we have already survived the end of a life as one which is beneath consideration?'[2] His own answer to that question we shall consider presently. Meanwhile we may further agree with McTaggart when he says: ' . . . it seems to me that, if we succeed in proving immortality, it will be by means of considerations which would also prove pre-existence. I do not see how existence in future time could be shown to be necessary in the case of any being whose existence in past time is admitted not to be necessary. If the universe got on without me a hundred years ago, what reason could be given for denying that it might get on

[1] Lotza, for example, treats it as a serious objection to a particular argument for immortality, that it would lead to the 'strange and improbable' conclusion of pre-existence: *Metaphysic*, Section 245. [McTaggart's footnote]

[2] J. M. E. McTaggart, *Some Dogmas of Religion*, Ch. IV, Section 86.

without me a hundred years hence? Or if it is consistent with my eternal nature that its temporal manifestation should begin at some point in time, could we find any reason for supposing that the cessation of that manifestation at some point in time would be inconsistent with that nature? I do not see of what kind such a reason could be, nor do I know of any attempt that has been made to establish one.'[1]

What I have tried to do in this section has been to express likewise a logical kinship between doctrine of a future life and pre-existence. I have tried to show that both these ways of talking about 'immortality' stand or fall together, and that the same logical cautions will be needed about each. At the same time, however, I would like to emphasise the point which McTaggart did not make clearly enough, if at all, that a doctrine of 'immortality' is *not* logically homogeneous with any doctrine of a 'future life'. Indeed, what I have suggested is that the old doctrine of pre-existence is just about as naive and mistaken as the old doctrine of future existence. Neither can be defended if taken as language suited to an immortality-claim while being descriptive of the 'objects' or 'observables' of another world before or after this. Equally, both can be defended if they are logically complex enough to be currency for that kind of disclosure-situation in which our 'immortality' is known. Following Dunne's suggestion, the new point raised by this section is that a better picture for both pre-existence and future existence and so for immortality may be one supplied by talk of a stratified personality extending forwards and backwards without end, talk which is then rightly complicated by doctrines of Creation and End, so as to make sure to emphasise not only our transtemporal existence, but the inadequacy of *any* serial story (whether backwards or forwards or both) if taken by itself to be the whole truth. For the doctrine of pre-existence, no less than all talk about a future life, has to be currency appropriate to a disclosure-situation of the kind we have repeatedly had in mind.

[1] *Ibid.*, Section 87.

B. The next theme on which we offer some brief reflections is *Universalism: Is everyone immortal?*

Our argument has been that we are immortal because there can be evoked personal situations not restricted to the spatio-temporal elements they contain. We have argued, for instance, that everybody who has at one time or another acted decisively, has in so doing realised their immortality. Two questions now seem to arise:

1. Have we to suppose, consequentially, a sort of intermittent immortality? Is such a supposition even meaningful?

To answer these questions, let us begin by considering a particular living organism A, which, though it was in every other way a human being, never at any time performed a de-liberate action; never at any time acted freely or responded to an obligation, and so on. Its life was one of instinct and 'habit'. Then there would certainly be *no reason* to call such an organism A_1 'immortal', as we have used that phrase, however, that an otherwise identical organism A_2, even on only one occasion, acted decisively or responded to an obligation, then, by so doing, A_2 would realise that about himself which exceeded the spatio-temporal; A_2 would know something which could not properly be said to begin or to end. So while, with the first case in mind, we might have *no* reason to say someone was 'immortal', or, with the second case in mind, *no immediate* reason to say someone was 'immortal', it would *not* however follow that A_1 and A_2 were not at all times transcendent and immortal. Some-one might be always both: yet only *aware of* his transcendence and immortality from time to time. Perhaps in some cases a man may never be aware of his immortality at all.

2. But (it might now be said) if in this way we cannot deny that everyone may be immortal, do we not commit the heresy of Universalism – that everyone will be saved?

Let us approach this second question by recalling that immor-tality evokes a situation which is subject-object in structure, that our immortality is known as we respond to some Other.[1] Let us

[1] Cp. pp. 98ff above.

also recall that some, such as McTaggart, have thought it sufficient to map this Other in terms of other people. So far the heresy of Universalism does not at all arise. For the heresy to arise we must at least go further and talk of the Other also in terms of God. The problem of Universalism then arises at the next move, if it is supposed that the granting of immortality to everybody implies some kind of limitation or restriction on God. But God is no more limited by everybody being 'immortal' in the sense in which we have explicated that term, than God's omnipotence is compromised by man's freedom.[1] As there is no problem in the one case, so there is no problem in the other. The old problem of universalism is solved by showing that a man's immortality and God's omnipotence – talked of best (as we saw) in terms of the power of God's love – are given together in one situation, precisely as God's omnipotence and human freedom are given.

c. So to our third and concluding theme: *What now has to be said about distinctively Christian claims?* What place can be given to Jesus Christ on the background of our discussion of immortality?

We may perhaps usefully start our discussion by recalling the question McTaggart raised in *Some Dogmas of Religion*: 'Why should men who are so anxious today to prove that we shall live after this life is ended, regard the hypothesis that we have already survived the end of a life as one which is beneath consideration?'[2] McTaggart's answer was that there is an anxiety to argue for immortality, while theories of pre-existence are neglected, because 'in modern western thought the great support of the belief in immortality has been the Christian religion. Under these circumstances a form of the belief which was never supported by that religion was not likely to be considered of any importance. And, for some reason, Christians have almost unanimously rejected those theories which placed pre-existence by the side of immortality, although there seems nothing in pre-existence

[1] Cp. pp. 56ff above.　　　　　　　　[2] See p. 139 above.

incompatible with any of the dogmas which are generally accepted as fundamental to Christianity.'

McTaggart is not alone in supposing that when the Christian declares his belief in 'eternal life' it is no more and no less than the philosopher's belief in 'immortality' or what we have seen to be logically very different, belief in a 'future life'. It was, for instance, A. A. Sykes who in 1720 in *The Principles and Connections of Natural and Revealed Religion,* declared that the resurrection of Jesus was 'an argument from eye-sight' for immortality. On the other hand, in more recent days, Christians have been so concerned to emphasise the distinctiveness of their belief in 'eternal life' as to dissociate it altogether from the philosopher's belief in immortality.[1] Where does the truth lie? Somewhere between the two extremes?

If our discussion of immortality is sound, then everyone, Christian or not, can reasonably believe in 'immortality'. They will further accept the possibility of talking about this 'immortality' (albeit guardedly) in terms of a future life, and they will agree with McTaggart that they can have no logical justification in refusing also to talk of it in terms of pre-existence.

To this point, there is nothing distinctive about the Christian position. Where then does the distinctively Christian claim arise? It certainly does not arise as a conclusion to an argument from analogy, though some Christian exposition comes dangerously near to suggesting this. The Christian must not argue: 'Jesus Christ lived again after death; we are like Jesus; therefore we will live after death too.' For, as C. D. Broad points out,[2] what is by no means obvious, but quite the contrary, is that we are 'like Christ'. All the same, it is in this kinship with Christ that the Christian hope centres, and we will now endeavour to give the Christian claim the elucidation it needs.

Christian belief in 'eternal life' is undoubtedly justified only by reference to a situation broadly similar to those to which we

[1] Cp. e.g. O. Cullmann, *The Immortality of the Soul,* London, 1958.
[2] See *Religion, Philosophy and Psychical Research,* pp. 236-7.

have been appealing all along. But the situation gains its distinctiveness by being evoked in relation to the elements of the Christian dispensation. We need, for instance, to ponder the biblical narratives, in which we shall find a theme which can be briefly outlined like this. In the Old Testament, we find God talked of as one who was always choosing and making decisions, to which a response was invited and expected; but such a response was often withheld or refused. The faithful remnant dwindled; dwindled indeed to one, when Jesus was crucified. The Christian then speaks of God acting again in and through Jesus, and to this activity, this power of 'grace' the Christian responds in 'faith'. Here is something 'extra' – 'additional' – to what is attributed to God in the Old Testament, and we might usefully express the point by talking of a distinctively Christian situation as a 'second-order' disclosure. So the Christian response is different from any other response to any other discernment – the response, for instance, of freedom to the claims of Duty, precisely but only because it is a response to that 'second-order' power and challenge which is displayed in Christ, Christ who was not only 'morally good' *but more besides*. So the Christian declares not merely that he believes in immortality, or even in eternal life, as we have hitherto used the term. These will be phrases which inadequately, and, indeed, misleadingly, express his claim; for they say nothing about its distinctive concern with Jesus Christ, nothing about its grounding in a second-order disclosure. A more apt expression of the Christian position is therefore more complex, being (so to say) a function of two variables – ordinary disclosure language on the one hand and a specific reference to Christ on the other. We speak, for example, of 'eternal life', *but* it is 'in Christ Jesus our Lord'. We 'live', we are 'free', *but* it is a 'life' and 'freedom' arising in relation to, and centred on Jesus Christ. This is the burden of such texts as 'alive unto God', *but* 'in Christ Jesus'.[1] 'I live and yet no longer just I, *but* Christ liveth in me.'[2] 'If therefore the Son shall make you free, ye shall be – (not only "free" but) free

[1] Rom. 6.11. [2] Gal. 2.20.

indeed.'[1] 'He that believeth on the Son hath eternal life.'[2]

The situation which these phrases describe is clearly *not* a plain 'immortality' situation, and to that extent McTaggart was misled and misleading. In fact, behind McTaggart's reflection is (I suspect) the belief that Christians, obviously admitting a time when a man consciously embraces 'eternal life in Christ Jesus', so that there is a time when 'eternal life' [*sic*] might be said to start, must in consequence talk of a start of 'immortality', in this way excluding from consideration any concept of pre-existence. That Christians like A. A. Sykes might have argued like this, is undeniable; that everyone who argues like this supposes 'immortality' and 'eternal life in Christ Jesus' to be in every way synonymous, is obvious. Yet such a supposition is quite mistaken. The Christian concern with the future rather than with the past, undoubtedly arises from its concern with 'eternal life in Christ Jesus'. But this is to be vigorously distinguished from its concern with 'immortality' – wherein it has nothing distinctive to say, and undoubtedly (as we have said above) McTaggart's earlier point stands, viz. that in so far as anyone (Christian or not) believes in immortality, he ought also to believe in pre-existence. 'Eternal life in Christ Jesus', then, does not talk of what 'immortality' talks of. On the other hand, it does not talk of a situation utterly different from the situation which justifies belief in immortality, and to that extent those who would altogether dissociate the philosopher's belief in immortality and the Christian belief in eternal life, over-argue their point. In fact, it is only because Christian phrases describe a situation similar in its broadest features to an immortality-situation, that the Christian can reasonably talk of his 'eternal life in Christ Jesus' in terms of language of the same logical brands as we have noticed above, talking, as he does for example in John 6.40 about 'the last day'. The Christian, in short, has his own stories of the End, his own particular purpose-stories, his own particular duty-stories, and his own special stories of love, stories suited to the situation which is central to his creed,

[1] John 8.36.   [2] John 3.36.

and because they are so suited, their logic must be even more complex than in the case of general talk about immortality. *Verb. sap.!*

And yet we must not be so overwhelmed by this complexity of Christian doctrine about 'eternal life in Christ Jesus our Lord' as to claim that nothing whatever can be done towards its logical mapping; that nothing whatever can be done to show its wider reasonableness, and its empirical grounding. The detailed prospect may be peculiarly complex and difficult, but that is not to say that we cannot formulate logical guides to some landmarks. In the case of an illustration,[1] we have seen already what light can be thrown on Christian language, and I conclude this section by taking those reflections a little further and broadening them into a general point.

The philosophical position I have set out in this book suggests plainly an emphasis on 'realised eschatology'. This technical theological phrase, roughly speaking, stands for the point of view that all talk about the Last Things has to be understood by reference to Jesus of Nazareth the Christ, in whose life and ministry and continuing presence were, and are, to be realised what has been traditionally expected as occurrences in the 'Last Days'. 'Realised eschatology' concentrates all the significance of Jesus Christ in a present situation by reference to which all doctrine, not least about the Last Things, must be understood. What, however, about 'future eschatology'? Is there nothing of the 'Last Things' to be given a 'future' reference? Does anything more need to be said?

We are now approaching in more general terms the point we made in more detail in our illustrative discussion of Dr Robinson's book, and I can express the more general point like this.

If we regard the logical structure of 'future eschatology' as correlative with 'realised eschatology', I do not think we do justice to either phrase. 'Future eschatology' has a different logic altogether. As we have seen, it must not be taken to describe some 'last occasion', some extra going-on which has yet to

[1] See pp. 122ff above.

146

come, as a substantial and impressive report may nevertheless have an appendix yet to be sent in. 'Future eschatology' for the Christian, like the concept of 'End' in the more general case, arises from an attempt to do full justice to the *total* character of the 'present' challenge in temporal terms. The phrase 'future eschatology' therefore is a convenient label for such supplementary language as endeavours to do full and clear justice to the distinctive kind of situation which the phrase 'realised eschatology' contrives to indicate. Thus, 'future eschatology' and 'realised eschatology' are not at all the correlatives which their grammatical form may seem to suggest. We have not two brands of eschatology. The one phrase provides us with a compact *label for the situation* which is 'eternal life in Christ Jesus our Lord'; the other phrase is a mnemonic, reminding us that without a certain *language* supplement relating to an 'End', all talk about that situation will be inadequate and misleading. The one phrase – 'realised eschatology' – belongs to a second-order disclosure-situation; the other phrase – 'future eschatology' – reminds us that a necessary part of the language needed to talk about that situation will include words like 'End' or 'Last Things', words whose logical behaviour (as we have seen) is misunderstood at our peril.

So to a final reflection. I started by saying that the title of this book might bring back to some readers memories of Kant. Perhaps indeed Kant has an importance and relevance for us for which he is not always given credit. While Kant might have been inadequate when he argued in *Religion Within the Limits of Reason alone*, that all Christian doctrine had to be understood in relation to our experience of Duty, yet I think Kant was abundantly right in so far as he suggested that even Christian doctrines only receive an adequate logical placing when they are given in relation to a situation which, in some very important respects, is similar to that in which we discern Duty. It is with situations of this kind that I have been specially concerned throughout the book, and in these last sections I have tried to indicate as well the relevance of our general consideration to the Christian claim. The distinctiveness of the Christian belief in 'eternal life in Christ Jesus' arises in relation to a situation which, while in its broadest respects is similar to an immortality-situation, is in other ways characteristically and importantly different.

In this chapter, then, I have tried to outline the kind of way in which the logical mapping of complex doctrines, like those of a future life, an End of history, and so on, might be developed. I have tried to show how the structure of these doctrines could be illuminated, and their empirical reference made more clear, if we brought alongside language of certain types, all of which was grounded – though in different ways – in a disclosure-situation.

If there is any one final moral I suppose it might be this: how cautious we have to be when we read off metaphysical, and especially Christian, claims! Let us never be misled by the all-too-obvious and all-too-misleading grammar of the phrases. Always, and especially in controversy, when the phrases seem nonsense, let us go back to the rock whence they were hewn – a disclosure-situation which is 'objects' and more, the kind of situation in which is founded all metaphysics, all religion, and – in a second-order disclosure – even the Christian faith itself. We shall indeed find theological discourse illuminating only when we read it as language suited to such a situation as that.

VI

RETROSPECT

IT MAY BE useful to the general reader if I list here some of
the main stages in the argument of the book:

1. From traditional discussions of predictability two contrary
claims can be filtered out:

(a) that human behaviour is no more than its scientifically-
describable features;

(b) that some human behaviour, i.e. a person's actual 'decisive' behaviour at a particular time, eludes complete
description in scientific terms.

(b) is the claim which is enshrined in the doctrine of 'free will'.

2. Ordinary language which does justice to the complexity
of 'decision' exhibits such a diversity as supports the wider of
the above alternatives.

3. But the situation to which the doctrine of free will appeals
is not only, and *subjectively*, a characteristic sort of *decision* in
which a person transcends his public behaviour; such a decision
occurs as a *response* to a challenge – called 'duty' or 'obligation' –
which, in a similar way, but *objectively*, transcends the observables through which it is expressed.

4. It is a logical howler to talk of this response in terms of
'causal determination'.

5. The transcendent challenge has been alternatively described by philosophers in terms of 'Duty' or 'God's will'; and
those who use the second phrase and justify it by its wider
empirical usefulness, are giving to 'God' a logical behaviour
modelled on the 'I' which is appropriate to a free-will situation

in its subjective aspect. But the logical structure of such language about God's will must not be misread, or it will lead to pointless confusion and bogus problems.

6. A similar reflection, viz. that the problem may have arisen from a logical misunderstanding, makes possible a new approach to the problem of freedom and omnipotence. We are precisely 'free' in that situation where we are able to speak of its objective challenge in terms of God's 'omnipotence'; freedom and omnipotence are no more incompatible than freedom and obligation.

7. To be 'free' as we have claimed it, is to be 'immortal', for it is to transcend the spatio-temporal. Not surprisingly, then, arguments for and against immortality respectively substantiate or deny the same claim which was at issue in arguments about unpredictability and predictability: that personal behaviour is not exhausted by all that object-language talks of.

8. Such phrases as 'immortality', 'eternal life', and 'timeless self', if they are to be unmistakably grounded in the kind of situation which it is the function of arguments for immortality to evoke, must be regarded as qualified models. In this way, they are given a logical structure suited to their topic.

9. The philosopher can welcome the contemporary Christian emphasis on the Hebrew use of the word 'soul', where the logical behaviour of 'soul' is closely similar to that of 'I' or 'person'.

10. All talk about immortality must be apt currency for a situation which no number of 'objects' ever exhausts. It cannot therefore be talk about objects alone; yet it must be talk about 'objects' if it is to be at all intelligible. An obvious suggestion is that (to combine adequacy with intelligibility) we use talk about a *never-ending* series of 'objects'. Here is the broad justification for talking of immortality in terms of a 'future life'. Stories of a 'future life' are thus to be understood by reference to a doubly-infinite series of moments, such as Whitehead has shown us how to construct. But this is a very approximate picture for a future life, not least because death seems to imply some sort of discontinuity.

I. Developing that point the next suggestion is that talk of a future life should trade in discontinuous time-periods: what in theological language is sometimes called 'aeons'.

II. Reverting, however, to the earlier possibility, and ignoring the difficulty about continuity beyond death, other possibilities arise for talk of a future life suited to what is meant by immortality. These possibilities occur when talk about a never-ending series is necessarily complicated and developed to make it clear beyond all doubt that such serial stories are currency for a 'more-than-objects' situation: that we are talking about the 'immortality' of persons and not the survival of a brick.

(*a*) The first method of complication attaches to the story of a future life, the concept of an 'End' whose logic is at least as complex as that of a mathematical 'limit'. To remember that is to recognise that the 'End' cannot be an event occurring at some moment of time, a reflection which has important implications for contemporary theology.

(*b*) The second method uses language about a future life which incorporates as basic units around which it is built, themes whose grounding in 'more-than-objects' situations is already recognised. We may take three examples:

  (i) talk of a future life in terms of purposiveness and progressive fulfilment;
  (ii) talk of a future life in terms of moral retribution – rewards and punishments;
  (iii) talk of a future life in terms of the characteristically personal virtue of *agape*.

Here then are some clues to logical areas which need to be distinguished within discourse about a future life if we are to see their characteristic claims, and to be alerted to possible confusions and misunderstandings.

11. The doctrine of pre-existence reminds us that immortality situations can also be talked of in terms of stories about the past. Taking up again the theme of discontinuity (10.I above) and following up Dunne's suggestion, we noted that one of the best pictures for immortality may be that of a stratified personality, extending backwards and forwards without end,

but surrounded by doctrines of Creation and the Last Things.

12. The old problem of Universalism is solved by showing that man's immortality and God's omnipotence are to be reconciled in the same way as earlier we reconciled man's freedom and God's omnipotence.

13. Christian belief in 'eternal life in Christ Jesus our Lord', is grounded in a situation importantly similar to one which justifies belief in immortality, but it has distinctive features which can be indicated by speaking of a second-order disclosure.

14. Behind the arguments lie at least three convictions:

(i) that ordinary language, like ordinary situations, if it is ordinary enough to extend to the Promenade at New Brighton, road accidents, disasters at sea, marriage, nicknames and the children's toys, exhibits such diversity as argues for the possibility of metaphysics, i.e. for the possibility of some language used aptly about what is 'unseen' (and what will still be 'unseen' tomorrow, whenever tomorrow is).

(ii) that no logical structure will be rightly assigned to a phrase in metaphysical theology unless it grounds that phrase in a disclosure-situation which includes observables and more than observables, what is seen and what is unseen. In other words, here is a necessary, though not a sufficient, condition for a phrase to be metaphysical.

(iii) that many puzzles and problems arise from logical misallocations, and that controversy is pointless unless and until the logic of the various claims is agreed. This is the case, for example, with the problem of free will, of freedom *versus* omnipotence, of the doctrine of the Last Things.

None of these convictions is in itself very startling or novel, but at least they register a protest against two popular misconceptions: that those with an intense affection for ordinary language must necessarily deny metaphysics, or that those who defend metaphysics must necessarily trade in occult realms and shadowy worlds. Which means that the book has been fighting on two battle-fronts at once; and it is a sobering reflection that not many wars have been won under such a necessity.

INDEXES

INDEX OF SUBJECTS

INDEX OF REFERENCES